THE **TESTING** SERIES

INTERVIEW
QUESTIONS &
ANSWERS

THE **TESTING** SERIES
expert advice on test preparation

Orders: Please contact How2become Ltd, Suite 2, 50 Churchill Square Business Centre, Kings Hill, Kent ME19 4YU.

You can order via the email address info@how2become.co.uk or through our main distributer Gardners Books at Gardners.com.

ISBN: 9781907558740

First published 2012

Typeset for How2become Ltd by Molly Hill, Canada.

Printed in Great Britain for How2become Ltd by Bell & Bain Ltd, 303 Burnfield Road, Thornliebank, Glasgow G46 7UQ.

CONTENTS

CHAPTER 1
INTRODUCTION   13

CHAPTER 2
MY FORMULA FOR SUCCESS   25

CHAPTER 3
SAMPLE INTERVIEW QUESTIONS AND RESPONSES   35

CHAPTER 4
OVERCOMING INTERVIEW NERVES   139

CHAPTER 5
THE COMMON INTERVIEW MISTAKES   141

CHAPTER 6
PLAN B   145

CHAPTER 7
BONUS SECTION. HOW TO CREATE AN EFFECTIVE CV   149

WELCOME

I have created this guide to help you pass your job interview. Competition right now for jobs is fierce; therefore, you need to be at your best. Within this book I have provided you with a large number of interview questions, tips on how to respond to those interview questions and also a large number of sample responses to help you prepare fully.

Within this section I have provided you with some invaluable tips on how to predict the types of questions you are likely to get asked at interview and I have also provided some new tips on how to predict the interview questions. If you know the interview questions, then your chances of success will increase greatly.

If you would like any further assistance with your preparation for any kind of job interview, assessment centre or selection process, then we offer a wide range or products and training courses at the website www.how2become. co.uk.

Finally, you won't achieve much in life without hard work, determination and perseverance. Work hard, stay focused and be what you want!

Good luck and best wishes,

The how2become team

The How2become Team

PREFACE BY RICHARD MCMUNN

For the vast majority of people, interviews are a nerve-wracking experience. At the very least, they are something that you could probably do without, right? This book is aimed at changing your entire mind-set towards interviews and more importantly, making you believe that success is in your own hands.

I have enjoyed a fantastic career during my life so far. I've been an Aircraft Engineer in the Royal Navy, an Officer in the Fire Service and now an entrepreneur and published author. I left school with very few qualifications but I was determined not to let this lack of educational achievement get in the way of being successful.

During my time in the Fire Service I passed many promotional interviews. I was successful at over 95% of interviews that I attended. My success wasn't down to luck, or some miracle 'interview success gene', but rather adopting the correct approach to both my interview preparation and also the interview itself. During this guide I will teach you how to implement my success formula into your own life. I suggest that you use it every time you go to interview.

The majority of people believe that you have to answer every interview question correctly in order to get the job. This couldn't be further from the truth. Yes it is important to demonstrate during an interview that you have both the subject knowledge of the role you are applying for, and also knowledge about the organisation you are applying to join, but it is just as important to work on your interview technique and your 'likeability' factor. When I interview people for roles within my company I will put more emphasis on their likeability factor rather than on their technical ability and their ability to respond to the questions. I am not saying that you should neglect these important areas, far from it. What I am saying is that you should portray yourself in a positive and enthusiastic manner during the interview. If you do, then your chances of success will improve.

What is the likeability factor?

The likeability factor could involve some or all of the following:

- Being polite and courteous at the interview.
- Displaying respect and good manners. I.e. not sitting down in the interview chair until invited to by the panel.
- Showing a high level of enthusiasm for the job you are being interviewed for.
- Taking a pride in your appearance.
- Showing a willingness to go above and beyond the minimum expectations.

I personally believe that we now live in an age where an uncomfortable number of employees believe he/she are doing the employer a favour by actually turning up to work. I am not saying this is the same for everyone, but I have witnessed a large number of people take too many days off sick and constantly moan about their job or the conditions they serve under. I personally don't vote for any political party, but I believe the Labour Government has a lot to answer for the attitude that some employees have. If you want to get a job you need to stand out from the crowd for the right reasons. My view is simple: a fair day's work for a fair days pay. Have a positive attitude when preparing for your job interview and be prepared to work hard; trust me, it pays off!

When I prepare for any interview I will always split my preparation up into three different areas. These are:

- Interview technique
- Research
- Responding to the interview questions

If I work on all of these three elements in equal measures then I will have the confidence and knowledge to pass the interview. When I walk through that door into the interview room I only have one thing on my mind – impressing the panel sufficiently that they will have to give me the job. During this guide I will teach you how to comprehensively cover all three of these areas.

So, you will probably be able to tell that my mindset, both prior and during the interview, is one of confidence and self-belief. These two factors are very important in helping you to pass the interview. By the time you've finished reading this guide you will have both of them, and in copious amounts too!

I strongly believe that passing interviews is like riding a bike – once you know how, it never leaves you. Take the time to study the contents of this guide carefully and then go and pass your interview with flying colours!

Best wishes,

Richard McMunn

DISCLAIMER

Every effort has been made to ensure that the information contained within this guide is accurate at the time of publication. How2become Ltd is not responsible for anyone failing their interview as a result of the information contained within this guide. How2become Ltd and their authors cannot accept any responsibility for any errors or omissions within this guide, however caused. No responsibility for loss or damage occasioned by any person acting, or refraining from action, as a result of the material in this publication can be accepted by How2become Ltd.

CHAPTER 1:
INTRODUCTION

Most employers are seeking people who are confident, reliable, enthusiastic, motivated, hard-working, committed and loyal. By understanding what an interview panel are looking for in a successful candidate you will be increasing your chances of success dramatically. Before I go into any interview I always try to put myself in the shoes of the interviewer. What are they looking for in an employee, what are the key qualities required to perform the role, and what does the job description say? Once I have the answer to these questions then I can start to prepare effectively for the interview.

WHAT IS AN INTERVIEW?

An interview is a tool used by the employer to assess a candidate's **potential** to perform a role. Unless you are an internal applicant who is seeking a promotion or sideways move, the interview will normally be the first time that the employer has the opportunity to meet you. They will want to assess whether or not you have the qualities to perform the role competently, the experience that you have so far in a similar role, and also whether they like you as a person and whether you are likely to fit into the team environment.

Many interviews will be structured around the fact that the interviewer will only assess you against your responses to the questions that are asked of you. This type of approach is more common for roles in the public sector. For example, when I interviewed candidates for positions in the Fire Service

I wasn't permitted to take into account what the interviewee was wearing. He or she could have turned up in jeans or trainers, but I wasn't allowed to take this into consideration when assessing the candidate's motivations for joining. Despite these restrictions any person who turns up to a job interview in jeans or trainers, unless specifically requested to, doesn't deserve to get the job. Why? Simply because I believe it shows a lack of motivation and commitment for the job, even before they've started.

A job interview is *your* opportunity to shine. It is your chance to show the employer that you *are* the person for the job and that you will do all that you can to perform above and beyond expectations if successful. Just by being at the interview you should naturally be enthusiastic about the prospect of working for the company. Why be there if your heart is not in it?

The psychological element of an interview is very important. Preparing emotionally for the interview is just as important as researching the company. Being in the right mindset will help you to perform at your best. There are many things that you can do to ensure you are in the right frame of mind, both immediately prior to the interview, and in the weeks and days leading up to it. Some of these include walking, running, swimming or general exercise, eating healthily and also avoiding alcohol or junk food. To the majority of people, these small changes won't seem worth the effort. However, through personal experience, these small changes can make a massive difference to your mindset and self-confidence.

MATCHING THE JOB DESCRIPTION AND/OR THE PERSON SPECIFICATION

Before you start preparing for the interview you must get a copy of the job description and person specification for the job you are applying for. The vast majority of employers will assess you primarily against these important documents. Your first task is to try to think of areas where you match the job description and person specification. You will see on the following page that I have provided you with a sample job description for a Customer Services Representative role. Following the job description you will notice that I have provided you with a number of 'key evidence areas'. These areas are the ones that I suggest a candidate who is being interviewed for this post focuses on during his or her preparation. It is vital that you can provide **evidence** of where you match the job description for the role that you are applying for.

CUSTOMER SERVICE REPRESENTATIVE – MAIN JOB TASKS AND RESPONSIBILITIES

- Deal directly with customers either by telephone, electronically or face to face
- Respond promptly to customer inquiries
- Handle and resolve customer complaints
- Process orders, forms, applications and requests
- Direct requests and unresolved issues to the designated resource
- Keep records of customer interactions and transactions
- Record details of inquiries, comments and complaints
- Record details of actions taken
- Manage administration
- Follow up on customer interactions

KEY EVIDENCE AREAS

- Provide examples of where you have dealt with customer queries and complaints in a professional manner. Make sure the example provided demonstrates that you have kept in contact with the customer and checked that they are fully satisfied with your resolution and service.
- Give examples of where you dealt with a customer quickly and competently. This might be where you have responded to a customer's request within a timeframe that is far shorter than the set standard.
- Provide more than one example of where you have processed a customer's order. Explain exactly what you did and how you followed company policies and procedures.
- Provide details of where you have recorded conversations with customers and also where you have kept an organised log of your dealings with them.
- Provide evidence of where you have followed up on a customer query. This demonstrates very good customer service.

HOW TO PREDICT THE INTERVIEW QUESTIONS

Is it really possible to predict the interview questions? The answer is yes. Here's how to do it:

Step 1 – Get a copy of the job description and person specification for the role you are applying for.

Step 2 – Grab a highlighter pen and 'highlight' the key requirements for the role.

Step 3 – You will now be able to predict the interview questions based on the key requirements for the role. For example, if one of the key requirements for the role is *'an ability to respond to customer complaints quickly and efficiently'*, the predicted interview questions for this key element are:

Q. Provide an example of where you have dealt with a customer's complaint from start to finish. What did you do and why?

Q. What is the process for dealing with a customer's complaint?

Q. What considerations would you take into account when dealing with customers complaints?

By following the above process you will easily be able to predict the interview questions for the role you are applying for. In order to make it easier for you I will now provide a practical demonstration using a job description for a sales manager. To begin with, take a look at the following job description.

JOB DESCRIPTION: SALES MANAGER

As a sales manager with our company you'll be organising and leading a team of sales representatives. You will also be responsible for a particular type of product or customer and be in charge of a particular geographical area.

YOUR RESPONSIBILITIES WILL INCLUDE:

- Setting sales targets for individual reps and your team as a whole, according to company guidelines.
- Recruiting and training sales staff.
- Allocating areas to sales representatives.
- Developing sales strategies and setting targets.
- Monitoring your team's performance and motivating them to reach targets.
- Compiling and analysing sales figures.
- Dealing with some major customer accounts yourself.
- Collecting customer feedback and market research.
- Reporting back to senior managers.
- Keeping up to date with products and competitors.

HOURS AND ENVIRONMENT

Normally, you'll work 9am to 5pm, Monday to Friday. However, you may have to work longer when necessary and there will be some weekend work as and when required.

You'll be office-based, but also spending some of your time visiting customers, head office, and your sales team in the field. You may also need to attend conferences, trade fairs and exhibitions.

SKILLS AND INTERESTS REQUIRED FOR THE ROLE

- Excellent sales and negotiation skills
- The ability to motivate and lead a team
- Initiative and enthusiasm
- Excellent communication and 'people skills'
- Good planning and organisational skills
- The ability to work calmly under pressure
- Good IT, budget and report writing skills
- A full driving licence
- Foreign language skills are increasingly useful.

From the above document I can easily predict the types of question I will get asked. Here's a list for you:

Q. Give an example of where you have successful led a team through a project or brief.

Q. Provide details of any managerial experience you have to date.

Q. Have you ever been responsible for a large team or geographical area? If so, what challenges did you face and how did you overcome them?

Q. Give examples of when you have set targets for members of a team and how you went about monitoring their progress.

Q. How would you carry out target setting for a member of your team?

Q. Describe a time when you had to carry out a performance appraisal for a member of your team?

Q. What qualities does an effective team leader require?

Q. When recruiting members of staff for your team what would you look for in an individual?

Q. How often would you train and supervise a new member of your team?

Q. How would you allocate tasks to individuals within your sales team?

Q. How would you deal with an individual within your sales team who was not meeting targets?

Q. How do you set targets for your team?

Q. Would you set 'easy to reach' targets or would you set targets that were impossible to achieve?

Q. What experience do you have of monitoring sales figures and what action would you take if your team was down on their targets?

Q. How would you reward a member of your team who was performing above and beyond expectations?

Q. What experiences do you have of dealing with major company accounts? Would you ever allocate these types of accounts to a member of your team? If not, why not?

Q. What are the pros and cons of market research?

Q. How would you carry out market research?

Q. How would you effectively transcend the results from your market research to your team?

Q. Who are our major competitors?

Q. What strategies would you implement in order to stay ahead of our major competitors?

Q. Are you prepared to work outside your normal contracted hours and is working at weekends an issue for you?

Q. Provide us with examples of how you have motivated a team?

Q. How do you organise your workload?

Q. How do you prioritise tasks in order to achieve your targets?

Q. Give us an example of when you have remained calm under pressure?

The above sample interview questions have been created by analysing the job description. I guarantee that at least 75% of the above questions will come up at interview for this role. So, the first step when preparing for your job interview is to get hold of a copy of the person specification and job description and start analysing them in order to predict the interview questions.

PERSONAL APPEARANCE

This carries far more weight than people think. First impressions are so important. It says a lot about who you are. Remember that you only get one opportunity to create a first impression. Unless it is specifically not required you should always dress in proper business attire such as a suit and tie or equivalent if you are female.

Your shoes must be clean too, and if you need a haircut, then get it done a few days before. I always advise people to prepare the night before the interview and lay everything out pressed and ready for the morning. Even down to your underwear, which sounds ridiculous, but it is all about limiting the stress that you will already be under on the day of your interview. The last thing you want to be doing is rushing around for your clothes or shoes on the big day only to find you threw away those smart shoes months ago. Be organised in your preparation!

TRAVELLING TO THE INTERVIEW

- How are you going to get to the interview?
- Do you know where you are going to park?
- Are the trains or buses running on time?
- Do you need a congestion charge ticket if the interview is in London?

These are all obvious questions but important nonetheless.

Again, it is all down to preparation. Remember to take a contact number with you just in case you are going to be late for the interview. Then you can call them well in advance to tell them you will be late due to a breakdown or traffic congestion. If you are travelling by car, don't wear your jacket. Hang it up on a coat hanger so that it is not creased when you arrive for the interview.

PUNCTUALITY

This can be related to the above subject but is still just as important. Make sure you leave with plenty of time to spare before your interview. It's far better to arrive an hour early than 5 minutes late! I usually arrive 30 minutes before my interview and sit in the car and re-read the job description for the role or information about the company that I am applying to join.

THE INTERVIEW FORMAT

Just by virtue of the fact you have been offered an interview indicates that the employer believes you have the potential to work for them in that particular role.

They will have already carried out a screening process based around the qualities and attributes relating to the post that you have applied for. The interview is designed so that the employer can see you in person and look at your demeanour, presence, personality and appearance along with the opportunity to ask you questions based around your application form and the role that you are applying for.

You may be competing against up to 30 applicants, so it is important that you stand out in a positive way and not for the wrong reasons. The basics of interview etiquette are key to your success, and you need to prepare for these as much as you do the interview questions themselves.

Most interviews will follow the following format:

Introduction and icebreaker

The interviewer should give you a brief overview of the interview and possibly the role that you are applying for. Dependant on the interviewer, you will be given the opportunity to tell the panel about yourself. Your response should be prepared beforehand and you can use this as an opportunity to sell yourself. You should cover brief topics relating to your experience, qualifications, outside interests and ambitions. If you tell the panel that in your spare time you are working towards a qualification that can relate to the role you are applying for then this can only be a good thing. Try to keep your introduction as brief as possible and don't go over two minutes in length.

The interview itself

This is the area in which you are asked a series of questions relating to your application form and the post that you have applied for. This is where you should do most of the talking and if you have prepared well enough you will be able to answer most questions, although it is not unusual to find yourself struggling to answer one or two. In this situation it is always best not to waffle. If you really don't know the answer to a particular question then just say so.

The opportunity to ask questions

This is a time for you to ask some questions to the panel. You should usually have two or three questions that you want to ask at the end. I have seen a few people fail interviews at this final stage. I can remember one particular person applying for a role as a firefighter. I was interviewing him for the role and he had answered all of the questions near perfectly. At the end of the interview I asked him whether he had any questions to ask the panel. Here's what he said:

"Yes I do have one question. How have I done? I personally think that I've had a fantastic interview and would I be very surprised if I've failed. Can I have feedback now please?"

The above question should never have been asked. It displayed arrogance and it also put the interview panel in an uneasy situation.

Make sure your questions are relevant but always avoid asking questions relating to leave or salary (unless you are specifically asked). Ask questions that relate to the role or development opportunities within the organisation. You may have researched the organisation and found that a new project is being developed. Ask them how the project is developing and what plans they have for the future. Don't ask questions where you are trying to be clever or questions that are too technical. If you try to catch them out they won't be impressed and they may come back and ask you a similarly difficult question.

Questions to ask

- If I am successful, how long will it be before I start training? (This shows enthusiasm and motivation.)

- During my research I noticed that you have just launched a new product. Has it been successful? (This shows a caring attitude towards the company, and also that you've carried out your research.)

- Even though I don't know yet whether I have been successful at interview, are their any books or literature I could read to find out more about the company? (This shows commitment.)

Questions to avoid

- How have I done during the interview? Have I passed? (This question demonstrates impatience and a slight level of arrogance. The interview panel will need to time to discuss your performance before making their decision.)

- How much leave will I get in this role? (I don't need to explain why this is a bad question!)

- How quickly can I progress through the company in terms of promotion? (This question, whilst demonstrating a level of enthusiasm, shows the panel that you have little intention of staying in the role long.)

- I have a holiday booked in four weeks time. If I am successful, can I have the time off? (You haven't even started and you are asking for time off. Wait until you have started in the role before discussing your leave requirements.)

The end of the interview

Make sure you remain positive at this stage and thank the entire panel for their time. This is a good opportunity to shake their hands. If you do shake their hand then make sure it's a firm grip and look them in the eye. There's nothing worse than shaking a person's hand when it feels like a wet lettuce!

At the end of every interview I always leave the panel with a final statement. Here's an example:

"I just want to say thank you for inviting me along to interview. I've really enjoyed the experience and I have learnt a tremendous amount about your company. If I am successful then I promise you that I will work very hard in the role and I will do all that I can to surpass your expectations."

This statement is very powerful. This is the final thing the interview panel will remember you for. When you leave the interview room they are probably going to assess/discuss your performance. Just as first impressions last, so do final impressions also.

CHAPTER 2:
MY FORMULA FOR SUCCESS

Over the last 20 years I have used the same formula time and time again to pass interviews. Over the next few pages and chapters I will explain what this formula involves, and more importantly how you can use it to assist you during every interview that you attend. The formula itself is a simple one, and is broken down into three different sections:

- Interview technique
- Research
- Responding to the interview questions

INTERVIEW TECHNIQUE

During my pre-interview preparation, I will concentrate on developing my interview technique. This will involve concentrating on the following key areas:

- Creating a positive first impression
- Presentation
- Effective communication

- Body language and posture
- Final questions
- Creating a positive final impression

Let's now break down each of these areas and look at them in detail.

CREATING A POSITIVE FIRST IMPRESSION

An interview panel will naturally create a first impression of you. As soon as you walk into the interview room they will be forming an opinion. Therefore, it is important that you get off on the right foot. Whenever I walk into any interview room I will always follow this process:

Knock before I enter the room

↓

Walk into the interview room standing tall and smiling

↓

Stand by the interview chair and say
"Hello, I'm Richard, pleased to meet you."

↓

Shake the hand of each interviewer firmly, whilst looking them in the eye

↓

Sit down in the interview chair, only when invited to do so

↓

Sit in the interview chair with an upright posture and with my hands resting palms facing downwards on the top of my knees, feet firmly on the floor

By following the above process I will be creating a positive first impression and demonstrating good qualities such as manners, self-discipline, politeness and motivation.

PRESENTATION

Presentation effectively means how I intend to dress for the interview, and also how I intend to come across. I want the interview panel to see me as a professional, motivated, conscientious and caring person who is taking the interview very seriously.

Some interviews, especially those in the public sector, do not require you to dress formally. For some bizarre reason, some senior managers believe that a person should not be assessed on how they present themselves at interview. Personally, I disagree with this approach. Whilst I agree there is no need to go out and buy an expensive suit or new pair of shoes, I do believe that a potential employee should make an effort in their appearance.

For the interview I will make sure that my suit is cleaned and pressed, my shoes are polished, and my personal hygiene is up to standard. This means simple things such as taking a shower, shaving, having a haircut and general grooming. I will always avoid brightly coloured clothes and generally go for a conservative approach such a dark blue, black or grey suit. If I do decide to wear any brighter, more vibrant colours, then this will be in form of a tie. I would strongly advise that you avoid brightly coloured socks or ties with cartoon characters on them!

A GOOD APPLICANT

A good applicant is someone who has taken the time to prepare. They have researched both the organisation they are applying to join and also the role that they are being interviewed for. They may not know every detail about the organisation and the role but it will be clear that they have made an effort to find out important facts and information. They will be well presented at the interview and they will be confident, but not overconfident. As soon as they walk into the interview room they will be polite and courteous and they will sit down in the interview chair only when invited to do so. Throughout the interview they will sit upright in the chair and communicate in a positive manner. If they do not know the answer to a question they will say so and they won't try to waffle. At the end of the interview they will ask positive questions about the job or the organisation before shaking hands and leaving.

A POOR APPLICANT

A poor applicant could be any combination of the following. They will be late for the interview or even forget to turn up at all. They will have made little effort to dress smartly and they will have carried out little or no preparation. When asked questions about the role they will have little or no knowledge. Throughout the interview they will appear to be unenthusiastic about the whole process and will look as if they want the interview to be over as soon as possible. Whilst sat in the interview chair they will slouch and fidget. At the end of the interview they will try to ask clever questions that are intended to impress the panel.

IMPROVING INTERVIEW TECHNIQUE

How you present yourself during the interview is important. Whilst assessing candidates for interviews I will not only assess their responses to the interview questions but I will also pay attention to the way they present themselves. A candidate could give excellent responses to the interview questions but if they present themselves in a negative manner then this can lose them marks.

EFFECTIVE COMMUNICATION

Effective communication is all about how you speak to the interview panel, and also how you listen to what they have to say.

When responding to the interview questions you should speak clearly and concisely, avoiding all forms of waffle, slang or hesitations such as 'erm'. Look at each interview panel member when answering each question. Even though an interview question will be asked by one member of the panel at a time, you should always respond to the entire panel collectively. Look them in they eyes when speaking to them but never stare them out. This will only portray you in an aggressive or confrontational manner.

If you are unsure about a response to an interview question then just be honest. Consider saying something along the lines of:

"I'm sorry I do not know the answer to that question. I will look the answer up as soon as I get back home and contact you to let you know the answer."

If they accept this response, make sure you do research the response and contact them to let them know.

When the interview panel are speaking to me, or if they are asking me a question, I will always demonstrate good listening skills. This means that I will use facial expressions to show that I am taking onboard what they are saying and I will also nod to show them that I understand the question(s).

BODY LANGUAGE AND POSTURE

Whilst sat in the interview I will always make a conscious effort to sit upright and not slouch in the chair. I personally like to use my hands to emphasise points when responding to the questions but I will be careful not to overdo it. Even if the interview is going great and you are building up a good rapport with the panel, don't let your standards drop. Always maintain good body language and posture for the duration of the interview.

FINAL QUESTIONS

Before I attend the interview I will always think of two questions to ask the panel at the end. However, don't be trapped in the thinking that you must ask questions. It is acceptable to say:

"Thank you but I don't have any questions. I have already carried out lots of research and you have answered some of my questions during the interview."

Some people believe that you must ask three, four or even five questions at the end of the interview – this is total nonsense. Remember that the interview panel will have other people to interview and they will also need time to discuss your performance.

If you do decide to ask questions then make sure they are relevant.

CREATING A POSITIVE FINAL IMPRESSION

I have already discussed this during a previous section. I believe that a final positive statement can work wonders:

"I just want to say thank you for inviting me along to interview. I've really enjoyed the experience and I have learnt a tremendous amount about your company. If I am successful then I promise you that I will work very hard in the role and I will do all that I can to surpass your expectations."

RESEARCHING THE ROLE AND THE COMPANY

I highly recommend you try to visit the company or organisation you are applying to join. This serves a number of purposes but the most important are demonstrating commitment and dedication to the potential employer but also assisting you in your preparation for the interview.

Other great ways to find out about a particular company are by visiting their website, if they have one. Look for their 'mission statement', 'goals or 'values' and try to learn them to understand what they are all about and where they are going. Another effective research method is to type the company's name into a search engine such as Google or Yahoo. This should bring up a number of links for you to research.

Make sure that the information you read is current and up to date, and don't waste time reading items that are more than a year old as you will most probably find that they have changed since then.

TOPICS YOU SHOULD RESEARCH

You can spend many weeks studying different topics, but the following areas should be a priority in your research plan:

- Do they offer any development programmes for their employees, e.g. Investors in People?
- When were they established?
- Is it a large company and do they have overseas interests?
- Who are their customers and who are their major competitors?
- Where are they located, who is their Chief Executive and who are the shareholders?
- What are their short, medium and longterm goals?
- What are their values and policies?
- What are their products?
- Do they have a mission statement or vision?

Top Tip
Only research things that are relevant and don't waste time reading irrelevant articles. Use your time wisely.

RESPONDING TO THE INTERVIEW QUESTIONS

The majority of interviews will contain two different types of questions. There will normally be motivational questions and situational questions. Here's an explanation as to how they differ.

MOTIVATIONAL QUESTIONS

Motivation interview questions are questions that are designed to assess the reasons why you want the job, what you have to offer, how much research you have done and also why you are the best candidate for the job. Whilst they are relatively easy to prepare for, you should still spend plenty of time getting your responses ready to the perceived motivational interview questions as these can, and often do, catch people out. Here's a list of sample motivational interview questions.

Q. Tell us a about yourself.

Q. Talk me through your CV.

Q. Why do you want this job?

Q. What do you have to offer?

Q. What skills do you have that would be of benefit in this role?

Q. Why should we give you the job and not the next candidate?

Q. I don't think you're experienced enough for this job. Convince me otherwise.

Q. What have you done to find out about this company and the role that you are applying for?

Q. How do you define success?

Q. What will you do if you are unsuccessful today?

You will see from the above list that the questions are very much aimed at your 'motivation' for wanting to join their company. Before you attend the interview I would suggest that you prepare responses for all of the above questions.

SITUATIONAL QUESTIONS

Situational interview questions are slightly harder to respond to. In order to determine the type of situational interview question you could be asked, I would recommend that you get a copy of the person specification or job description for the role. Once you have this to hand, you will then be able to prepare responses to the type of situations that you will be expected to perform within the role. The key to scoring high during your responses to this type of questioning is to provide evidence of where you have already been in this type of situation.

The following list of situational interview questions are ones that I recommend you prepare for.

Q. Give an example of where you have worked as part of a team to achieve a difficult goal or task.

Q. Give an example of where you have provided excellent customer service.

Q. Give an example of where you have dealt with a customer complaint. What did you do and say?

Q. Give an example of where you have carried out a task despite pressure from others.

Q. Give an example of where you have made a difficult decision despite objection from other people.

Q. Give an example of where you have taken onboard constructive criticism.

Q. Give an example of where you have dealt with a difficult or aggressive customer.

Q. Give an example of where you have resolved an issue with a work colleague.

STAR METHOD

The STAR method is one that I have used during my preparation for many interviews in the past. It works most effectively when preparing responses to situational type interview questions. I would certainly recommend that you try using it.

The STAR method basically ensures that your responses to the interview questions follow a concise logical sequence and also that you cover every possible area. Here's a break down of what it actually means:

Situation – At the commencement of my response I will explain what the situation was and who else was involved. This will be a relatively comprehensive explanation so that the interviewer fully understands what it is I am trying to explain.

Task – I will then explain what the task was. This will basically be an explanation of what had to be done and by whom.

Action – I will then move on and explain what action I specifically took, and also what action other people took.

Result – I will finally explain what the result was following my actions. It is important to make sure that the result was positive as a result of your actions.

Have a go at using the STAR method when creating responses to the perceived interview questions. Write down the question at the top of a sheet of paper and write down each individual element underneath it.

CHAPTER 3:
SAMPLE INTERVIEW QUESTIONS AND RESPONSES

Within this section of the guide I will provide you with lots of sample interview questions. Following the majority of questions I will provide you with a sample response to help guide you in the right direction. I have also provided you with a blank template following many of the questions, which I suggest you use to create your own response to each question. This will make sure that you cover every eventuality, and it will also prepare you far more effectively for your forthcoming interview.

WARM-UP QUESTIONS

These types of questions are usually asked at the beginning of an interview. They are sometimes used by an interview panel to give you the opportunity to warm up in preparation for the assessable questions.

Q. How was your journey here today?

This question is very easy to answer. However, avoid single word or short replies such as:

"Yes it was good thanks."

Try to add more substance to your response and use it as an opportunity to talk to the panel and also show them that you have some great qualities such as organisation and preparation.

"Yes it was a good journey thanks. I've never been to this building before so I carried out a dummy run last night. The last thing I wanted was to be late for the interview so I made sure that I prepared fully. I got up early this morning, checked the travel news and then set off with plenty of time to spare. I arrived here 30 minutes early so I sat in my car, composed myself and re-read my notes about the job and your company."

Q. Why have you decided to apply for this job?

This again is a very common interview question and one that needs to be answered carefully. Remember that an interview panel will have heard all of the usual responses such as "I've wanted to work in this kind of role since I was a child", and "This job just really appeals to me". These types of standard responses will gain you few marks.

It is crucial that you provide a response to this type of question that is unique, truthful and different to all of the other candidates.

Consider the following points:

- Provide a response that demonstrates you've carried out plenty of research. During your research something has caught your eye about the job that is very appealing. This will demonstrate to the panel that you have looked into the role. Remember that most candidates will apply for many different jobs all at one time, and as a result they will fail to carry out any meaningful research.

- Consider providing a response that demonstrates you have the key skills required to perform the job competently. An example would be:

"I understand that this role requires very good communication and team working skills. I believe I am very strong in these areas, and therefore I would be a valuable asset to the team. Having researched the job and organisation extensively I have noticed a common theme appearing time and time again – professionalism. I have also spoken to people who already work within this team, and the feedback I have received has been excellent.

I really want to work for this team and the skills and experience I have already gained will allow me to contribute towards the organisation's goals in a positive manner."

Warm-up questions can come in any format. The main aim for you is to make sure that you speak and communicate with the panel. Always avoid single word answers or short responses. The easy questions are your opportunity to get warmed up, and they are also your chance to create a rapport with the interviewers.

We will now take a look at a number of main interview questions.

QUESTION 1 – TELL ME ABOUT YOU?

This is a common introductory question that many interviewers use to break the ice. It is designed to get you talking about something you know – You!

A big mistake usually made by the majority of people is that they focus on their family, children, hobbies or home life. Whilst you may have some interesting facts about your personal life you should either avoid these, unless specifically asked, or keep them very brief. Try to answer this type of question based around your own personal achievements, educational background and ongoing studies. It is good to say that you are motivated or enthusiastic but you MUST ensure that you provide examples or scenarios where this has been proven. For example you might say, *"I am a motivated person – whilst working for my previous employer I achieved 'XYZ', which enabled the company to achieve its goal in relation to increased profit margins etc."*

Giving specific, brief examples is positive. Remember that anyone can tell an interview panel that they are 'motivated', 'enthusiastic' or 'determined' but not everybody can prove it. Try to think about and use some of the following key words when structuring some of your answers:

- Motivated
- Self-starter
- Responsible
- Enthusiastic
- Dedicated
- Committed

- Reliable
- Trustworthy
- Initiative
- Team player
- Organised
- Focused

It is also a good idea to think of occasions where you have initiated projects or ideas at work, which have gone on to achieve results.

There now follows a sample response to this question. Once you have read it, use the template on the following page to create your own, based on your own individual situation:

"My strong points are that I am focused, enthusiastic and dedicated. For example, whilst working for my current employer I was successful in achieving my annual appraisal sales target with 4 months to spare.

I like to ensure that I maintain a healthy balance between my personal and professional life. This helps me to maintain a high level of performance at work.

I recently embarked on a Diploma course, which I am now halfway through. I enjoy new challenges and like to take care of my own self-development.

I am an active person and enjoy visiting the gym 4 times a week. Some of my other hobbies include art, walking and cooking.

I am a caring person and when I have the spare time I try to get involved in community events in my local town. I recently ran a half marathon raising £450 for a local charity.

Overall I would say that I am a reliable, self-conscious and hard-working person who always looks for ways to improve."

Top Tip
Take any literature or evidence that you have along with you to the interview to prove to the panel that you are genuine.

TEMPLATE FOR QUESTION 1 – TELL ME ABOUT YOU?

QUESTION 2 – HOW WAS YOUR JOURNEY HERE TODAY?

This question is again an icebreaker. I have used it on many occasions during the initial questioning stage of interviews. This is an opportunity for you to engage with the interview panel, and also show them that you are organised and motivated. Whilst it is a very simple question to answer, there is an opportunity here for you to show them some of the qualities that you posses.

Take a look at the two sample responses to this question:

SAMPLE RESPONSE 1

"Yes I had a good journey thanks."

SAMPLE RESPONSE 2

"Yes the journey was fine thank you very much. I planned the journey a couple of days ago, just to make sure I knew exactly where I was going. The last thing I wanted was to be late. I got up early enough to check the travel details and arrived 30 minutes before the interview, just so that I could compose myself and read up, in my car, some information about your company and the role."

You will see that the second response is far more comprehensive. It also tells the interviewer that the candidate is organised, disciplined, motivated and conscientious. These are all good qualities that an employer would appreciate.

Now use the template on the following page to construct a response based on how you would personally answer the question.

TEMPLATE FOR QUESTION 2 – HOW WAS YOUR JOURNEY
HERE TODAY?

QUESTION 3 – WHAT HAVE YOU LEARNT ABOUT THIS COMPANY?

This question is extremely common during job interviews. Again, it is one that I have used time and time again when interviewing candidates for posts. I would personally expect an interviewee to have researched the organisation thoroughly before they come to interview. If you take onboard my advice in the earlier pages of this guide then you will be able to answer this question with relative ease. Try to state who their major competitors are, understand the vision and expectations of the company, and know internal information on the size, structure and organisation of the company.

Your research is paramount to your success and shows that you haven't just turned up on the day to make the numbers up. By learning all you can about the company, their products and services, you will demonstrate a commitment before you have begun.

SAMPLE RESPONSE TO QUESTION 3

"In the build up to the interview I carried out lots of research about your organisation. I found out that there are 70 staff who work for the company in various roles, from customer service representatives to senior managers. The Head Office is centred in Reading, but the majority of business is carried out at the 26 retail stores you operate throughout the UK, in counties such as Kent, Lancashire, Berkshire and Yorkshire. The company has a very good reputation for delivering high quality services, and as a result, has received awards at a national level for delivering excellence. It has also received Investors in People status. I am a professional and skilled person who would love to work in a company like yours, which constantly strives to improve and deliver excellence."

Now use the template on the following page to construct a response based on your research and centred on the company you are applying to join.

TEMPLATE FOR QUESTION 3 – WHAT HAVE YOU LEARNT
ABOUT THIS COMPANY?

QUESTION 4 – WOULD YOU SAY THAT YOU ARE A FLEXIBLE PERSON?

This question is designed to see if you are flexible in relation to working hours and also your level of commitment as an employee? It is an indication that the job or role that you are applying for requires you to work extra hours or that the company will rely on you to be available when required within reason.

The obvious and most appropriate answer to this question would be 'Yes'. It is then best to follow your answer up with evidence that you are flexible. You may have been required to be flexible in your previous post or job and therefore you can give examples to demonstrate your flexibility.

There now follows a sample response to this question. Once you have read it, use the template on the following page to create your own, based on your own individual situation:

"Yes I am very flexible and I fully understand that the role will require me to be available when required. In my previous job I made the manager aware that I was available to work extra hours if required. On one particular occasion I volunteered to stay behind after work to take delivery of some stock. The delivery driver was stuck in traffic and he called to say that he would arrive at 6pm, two hours later than scheduled. Even though it was a Friday afternoon, I realised how important it was that the delivery was accepted. I stayed behind, took delivery of the stock and checked the contents before locking up and going home."

TEMPLATE FOR QUESTION 4 – WOULD YOU SAY THAT
YOU ARE A FLEXIBLE PERSON?

QUESTION 5 – WHAT ARE YOUR STRENGTHS?

This is an extremely common interview question and one that you must prepare for. When answering this type of question I would advise that you give work-related examples. You should try to think of at least three good strengths that you possess, and provide an example of when you have used those strengths.

You may be able to give an answer along the following lines:

"One of my strengths is that I have the ability to implement change in difficult circumstances. For example whilst working for my previous employer I implemented a new policy under difficult and adverse conditions. The team were not happy with the changes that were being implemented, but I managed to motivate them by holding regular updates and team meetings. I have the ability to understand that the needs of the company will always come first. My strengths include an ability to inspire and motivate a team, as and when required."

This type of answer demonstrates to the panel that you are able to prove your strengths as opposed to just saying that you have them. Anyone can say that they are motivated, enthusiastic, dedicated or reliable, but proving that you have those strengths is a different matter.

Being able to demonstrate that you have strengths will give you higher scores.

Use the template on the following page to create your own response, based on your own individual strengths.

TEMPLATE FOR QUESTION 5 – WHAT ARE YOUR
STRENGTHS?

QUESTION 6 – WHAT ARE YOUR WEAKNESSES?

Possibly the worst answer you can give for a question of this nature is that you don't have any weaknesses. Being able to identify that you have weaknesses is a strength in itself. Obviously it is important that you answer this question carefully as you could reduce your chances of success if you portray yourself in a negative light. For example, if you are applying for a job as a mechanic and you are always losing your tools then you're probably not the right person for the job!

Here's an example of a response to this type of question:

"In my previous job I found it difficult to delegate work to others. I can be a bit of a perfectionist at times and I like a job or task to be done correctly to a high standard. Unfortunately this lack of trust caused problems within my team and a member of staff approached me to tell me they were not happy with the way I was working. I took their comments onboard and decided to ask the rest of the team if they felt the same. The feedback I received was along the same lines – that the majority of people felt I should delegate more work and responsibility to them. Following this feedback I decided to change my style of approach and began to delegate more work, placing greater trust on my colleagues. This had a very positive effect and the workload increased dramatically as a result of this change. Morale within the team improved too and now I hold regular feedback meetings with my colleagues to see how we can improve."

This type of response identifies that you have a weakness, but also identifies a number of strengths. It shows that you have the ability to look at yourself and make changes where needed. Accepting constructive criticism is one thing, but doing something about it is another. This also leads on to another possible 'strength' quality in the fact that you can identify your weaknesses and do something about them.

Here's another example of how this type of question might be answered.

"Yes I do have one weakness. If somebody is late for a meeting or an appointment I usually have to say something to them when they do eventually arrive. This can sometimes be taken the wrong way. I personally don't like lateness, but I am trying to understand that some people are just late as a rule and I have to be accepting of others."

This response is again demonstrating that you have a strength that most employers cherish – punctuality. The key to responding to this type of question is making your 'weakness' a 'strength'.

Use the template on this page to create your own answer to this question based on your own individual weaknesses.

TEMPLATE FOR QUESTION 6 – WHAT ARE YOUR WEAKNESSES?

QUESTION 7 – DO YOU ENJOY WORKING IN A TEAM ENVIRONMENT?

The answer to this type of question depends on the type of job you are applying for. If you are applying for a team role then obviously you need to answer this in a manner that shows you are a team player. Conversely if you are applying for a position that involves a lot of 'lone working' then it is a good idea to say that you feel comfortable working on your own. Possibly the best answer for this type of question is to state that you are adaptable and can work in any environment. Again, if you can give examples of situations where you have been an effective team member or achieved results independently then this is far better.

"In a previous role I was required to work as part of a 30-strong sales team. I really enjoyed the atmosphere within that team and managed to learn so much from other members. Yes I do enjoy working in a team environment but conversely my adaptability allows me to work in any environment. I would say that I can work either as one of a team or an individual depending on the requirements of the role. If I am required to work as part of a team then I will always listen carefully to the provided brief, keep in communication with the other team members, support those people who need supporting in the team, and also learn from any mistakes that the team makes so that we can improve next time.

I can remember one particular occasion when I was required to work as part of a team. Sales figures for the month were low and we were required to work as a team in order to generate new business leads. We all came together as a team and discussed the different options available to us. My role within the team was to source potential new clients over a two-week period whilst others sent out promotional materials once I had created the new leads. As a team we managed to increase sales and revenue by 50% in just a short space of time."

Use the template on the following page to create your own answer to this question based on your own experiences.

TEMPLATE FOR QUESTION 7 – DO YOU ENJOY WORKING
IN A TEAM ENVIRONMENT?

QUESTION 8 – ARE YOU A RISK TAKER?

A tricky question to answer but it all depends on the type of company or organisation you are applying to join. If the company is a well-established, steady organisation that has achieved its success over a long period of time, building a reliable name for itself, then it is wise to veer on the side of safety and state that you are not a great risk taker.

However, if the company of organisation has recently started up and is competing in a highly competitive industry then a level of risk taking may be commensurate to this role. If you do decide to say that you are a risk taker then it is a good idea to give examples of calculated risks that you have taken. Make certain that you emphasise that you would not take a risk unless you were positive of a successful outcome, and that you would never jeopardise the company. It is always best to seek advice from Senior Managers if unsure and this is something that you would always do unless you were certain of the outcome.

SAMPLE RESPONSE FOR A COMPANY/ROLE THAT REQUIRES A LEVEL OF RISK-TAKING

"If the situation requires then I am not averse to taking risks. However, the risks that I do take are always carefully thought through and focused on achieving the goal. I would always look, wherever possible, to consult my manager before taking the risk. In a previous role I was required to take risks on a weekly basis. However, those risks were always carefully calculated and veered on the side of caution. With regards to Health and Safety matters I would never take any risks and I would certainly never breach confidentiality."

SAMPLE RESPONSE FOR A COMPANY/ROLE THAT DOES NOT REQUIRE A LEVEL OF RISK-TAKING

"No I don't take risks, especially when work is involved. I always follow company rules and procedures and if I'm ever unsure of something I will always seek clarification first from a line manager or senior member of the team. I've seen people take risks at work before, and they usually end up going wrong. In terms of Health and Safety, I would never take risks. I would hate to be part of a situation at work where a member of the team became injured because somebody was taking risks or shortcuts. If I witnessed somebody doing something that they shouldn't be doing, then I would have to say something and inform my supervisory manager."

Now use the template on this page to create your own answer to this question based on your own opinions and beliefs.

TEMPLATE FOR QUESTION 8 – ARE YOU A RISK TAKER?

QUESTION 9 – WHAT ARE YOU LIKE AT TIME MANAGEMENT?

Time management is undoubtedly a skill not everyone possesses. Being able to manage your time effectively is not easy but there are some great ways of demonstrating your time management qualities. When you get into work, do you already know what you are going to achieve by the end of the day? During the final 30 minutes of your working day do you plan the following day's activities and tasks in order of priority? Do you keep a list of important objectives and tasks and cross them off when they are completed? If you are chairing meetings then do you keep irrelevant discussion to an absolute minimum and always ensure you finish on time? Are you acutely aware of others' valuable time as well as your own and do you make certain that time is not wasted unnecessarily?

The company's objectives are key to your time management. The above information gives you a number of time management tools to use when constructing your answer. It is also important to remember to emphasise that you are flexible with your time when needed, and that you reorganise appointments, meetings or tasks in order to meet specific important deadlines.

"I am very effective at time management. I am the type of person who is extremely organised and knows what they want to achieve during each day. I like to keep lists, which act as a reminder of what I want to achieve and in what timeframe. For example, if I have a busy schedule planned for the forthcoming week, I will always write down what I want to do during that week, the week before. This allows me to plan ahead and also makes sure that I have everything in place so that I can achieve each objective. I fully understand that the role I am applying for will require me to be competent at time management, and I am fully prepared for this."

Now use the template on the following page to create your own answer to this question based on your own skills, qualities and experience.

TEMPLATE FOR QUESTION 9 – WHAT ARE YOU LIKE AT
TIME MANAGEMENT?

QUESTION 10 – WHAT ARE YOU LIKE AT TAKING CRITICISM FROM SENIOR MANAGERS?

Regardless of how you think you would react, it is important to tell the interview panel that you look at this in a positive manner. Of course you do not want to portray an image that you are a pushover, but an answer along the following lines would be acceptable:

"Whilst working for my current employer, a situation arose where I was criticised for a mistake. At the time of the criticism I felt disappointed in my own performance, but knew it was important to learn from my mistake and improve for next time. I understand that not everybody is perfect and when we make mistakes it is the ability to move on and improve for next time that is important. I spoke with my line manager after the mistake was made, apologised and made certain I improved my performance in that particular area."

The above type of response identifies that you have the ability to accept criticism but also that you are sensitive to it too. Nobody likes criticism of any kind but in this response you have shown that you did not get angry, defensive or arrogant but instead you turned a negative situation into a positive one.

Now use the template on the following page to create your own answer to this question based on your own skills, qualities and experience. Try to think of a situation where you made a mistake, and provide an example of what you did to improve. When constructing your response try to include words such as 'reflect' and 'evaluate'.

TEMPLATE FOR QUESTION 10 – WHAT ARE YOU LIKE AT
TAKING CRITICISM FROM SENIOR MANAGERS?

QUESTION 11 – HOW WOULD YOU RESOLVE A DISPUTE WITH A WORK COLLEAGUE?

Everybody has disputes with colleagues at some point in their career so it is not wise to say that you've never had one. You may get on with the majority of people most of the time but it is good to say that you had an issue with a colleague years ago and describe how it was resolved. You could state that you were the one who initiated the resolution by talking to the other person to try to clear the air. This is a good opportunity to demonstrate you have good communication skills and are prepared to listen to what others have to say.

Maybe you took the colleague's comments onboard and agreed a way forward? It is a good idea to show that you are able to resolve issues with other colleagues without involving senior or line managers. However, if the dispute was in contravention to the company's policies on bullying or harassment then you would feel it was important to report the incident to your line manager.

"The first thing I would do is try to arrange a meeting with them; somewhere out of the way of any distractions, and in private. I would ask them if we could both search for ways to resolve our differences, with a view to possibly becoming friends or at the very least amicable work colleagues. It is only natural that we cannot get along with everybody; however, whilst at work we should put our differences aside and work towards the company objectives. I would do all that was in my power to resolve any conflict and I would never allow it to deter from my professionalism."

Now use the template on the following page to create your own answer to this question based on your own opinions and experiences. If you have already been in this type of situation before, explain how you resolved it.

TEMPLATE FOR QUESTION 11 – HOW WOULD YOU
RESOLVE A DISPUTE WITH A WORK COLLEAGUE?

QUESTION 12 – WHAT WOULD YOU DO IF YOU WITNESSED A WORK COLLEAGUE BEING BULLIED OR HARASSED?

There is only one correct answer to this type of question, and that is you must take action to stop it from occurring. If you cannot stop it then you should inform your line manager immediately. Make sure you say that you would follow company policy and always try to be sensitive to the needs of the person who is being bullied. You would probably need to take the time to talk to the person who is on the receiving end of such behaviour, and support/comfort them. Dependant on their wishes, you would consider informing their line manager.

It is important to say to the interviewer that you would read the company's policy on bullying and harassment. If you can obtain of copy of this before the interview, then it is good practice to read it. Always remember that this type of behaviour is not tolerated, both in society and in employment. The employer has a responsibility under law to prevent such behaviour. To read more guidance about how to deal with bullying and harassment in the workplace, please visit:

HTTP://WWW.ACAS.GOV.UK

"To begin with, I would certainly take some form of action. Bullying or harassment should never be tolerated in the workplace. I would make sure that I am conversant with the company's policy before taking action. However, I would do all that I could to stop the inappropriate behaviour, and that might involve informing a senior manager. I would speak to the person who was being bullied or harassed and do all that I could to support them. Sometimes those people who are acting as the bully do not realise what they are doing, and the impact of their actions. Therefore it is important to challenge the person who is carrying out the inappropriate behaviour."

Now use the template on the following page to create your own answer to this question.

TEMPLATE FOR QUESTION 12 – WHAT WOULD YOU DO
IF YOU WITNESSED A WORK COLLEAGUE BEING BULLIED
OR HARASSED?

QUESTION 13 – HAVE YOU EVER HELD A POSITION THAT WASN'T RIGHT FOR YOU?

The only right answer for this kind of question is 'no'. The problem with answering it with a yes is that you would have to explain how you ended up getting a job that wasn't right for you in the first place! Don't give the interviewer any reason to think that the job you are applying for is either out of your depth or wrong for you.

"No I have never been in that position. I am always very careful about the jobs that I apply for. I don't believe it would be fair on either myself or the company I was applying to join if I got a job that wasn't right for me. For instance, I know that this job is the right one for me. I have carried out extensive research into this role and also visited the company prior to the interview to ensure that, if I am successful today, then I will be both good at the job and good for the organisation."

Now use the template on the following page to create your own answer to this question. When creating a response to this question, try to provide the panel with examples of your skills and experiences that match the job description or person specification.

TEMPLATE FOR QUESTION 13 – HAVE YOU EVER HELD A
POSITION THAT WASN'T RIGHT FOR YOU?

QUESTION 14 – WHERE DO YOU SEE YOURSELF IN FIVE YEARS TIME?

This is an extremely common question amongst interview panels. Be careful how you answer this one though. I have been on interview panels where people say 'I don't know, I'll see what happens.' This is not a very good response to this question and displays a lack of ambition and drive.

I have also been on interview panels where people have given responses such as:

"I want to be sat in your seat doing your job."

Whilst I don't disbelieve them I feel that this type of response displays arrogance rather than confidence.

Try to structure your answer in a way that shows you are positive about the future but not overconfident. A good answer to use might be along the following lines:

"I believe I am the right person for this job. If successful I would like to further develop my skills and knowledge by initially learning all I can about the role and the organisation. I would also like to enrol on an educational programme in order to develop my skills and work towards a higher position within the company. Above all I will be looking to have developed both personally and professionally during that time."

Now use the template on the following page to create your own answer to this question. When creating your response, try to display a level of ambition, drive and a desire to personally and professionally improve.

TEMPLATE FOR QUESTION 14 – WHERE DO YOU SEE
YOURSELF IN FIVE YEARS TIME?

QUESTION 15 – IF YOU ARE SUCCESSFUL AT INTERVIEW, HOW LONG DO YOU PLAN STAYING WITH OUR COMPANY?

When responding to this question you need to imply that you intend on staying with the company for a long time. It is pointless an organisation investing time, effort and resources into your training and development if you do not plan on staying with them. You have identified that this is the company you want to work for, and therefore you want to commit your future to them.

All the time you are contributing effectively towards the company's desired achievements then you will be a part of them. If you say that you only plan to stay with them for a few years before moving on then they are unlikely to employ you. They want to know that they are going to get a substantial return for their investment.

"I have looked into both this role and the organisation. I have been impressed with the ambitions and plans that the company have. With that in mind I plan to stay with you for a long time if I am successful. Furthermore, I am serious about my application for this position and excited about the prospect of working with you. I understand that you are going to be investing a lot of time, money and resources into my development and I would intend repaying that investment by being a loyal and competent employee."

Now use the template on the following page to create a response to this question that is based on your own opinions and beliefs.

TEMPLATE FOR QUESTION 15 – IF YOU ARE SUCCESSFUL
AT INTERVIEW, HOW LONG DO YOU PLAN STAYING WITH
OUR COMPANY?

QUESTION 16 – WHY DO YOU WANT TO LEAVE YOUR CURRENT EMPLOYMENT?

This is a question that needs to be answered very carefully. It is not a good idea to state that you are leaving because of differences with a manager or member of the team. It is far better to say that you are looking for new and fresh challenges and feel that you have achieved all that you can at the company. The last manager that I worked under during my time in the Fire Service was, in my opinion, the worst boss I have ever worked for. However, I would never state that opinion during any future interviews or job applications. It is sometimes best to keep your personal views to yourself.

Most people want a higher salary but it is also not a good idea to use this as a reason for your intention to move organisations. By stating you would like a new challenge you will demonstrate drive and enthusiasm.

"Although I enjoy my current job I am now ready for a new challenge. I have worked hard for my previous employer and they have been good to me in return. I have learnt an awful lot during my time with them but I am now in a position where I want to embark on new and fresh challenges. I will be leaving my current company with fond memories but I know the time is right for me to move on.

Having looked into your company and the role that I'm applying for I feel that I have so much to offer in terms of my experience, drive and enthusiasm and know that I would be a valuable asset to the team."

Now use the template on the following page to create a response to this question that is based on your own views and opinions.

TEMPLATE FOR QUESTION 16 – WHY DO YOU WANT TO
LEAVE YOUR CURRENT EMPLOYMENT?

QUESTION 17 – WHY SHOULD WE GIVE YOU THE JOB?

You need to give the interview panel an answer that benefits them and not just yourself. Yes of course you are the best person for the job, but don't say it unless you can back it up with examples of why. Here are a few example of why you might be the best person for the job:

- You have the ability to work in a fast-changing environment that requires commitment, drive and enthusiasm.

- You are capable of achieving great things for their organisation and thrive under pressurised situations. For example in your previous role you were given a deadline of three days to achieve a highly complex task that required a high level of motivational skills to get the task completed on time. You brought the team together, briefed them on what was expected and monitored each stage of progress carefully.

- You can make a positive impact on sales/profit or turnover and are dependable in every situation to deliver what is required.

- You are a team player who has the experiences and skills to match the job description.

- You are loyal, hard-working and will act as a positive role model for their organisation.

This type of question can make or break you and you should be prepared with a hard-hitting positive response. Be enthusiastic when responding and give brief examples of why you are the right person compared to the next candidate.

Now use the template on the following page to create your own response.

TEMPLATE FOR QUESTION 17 – WHY SHOULD WE GIVE
YOU THE JOB?

QUESTION 18 – I AM CONSIDERING GIVING THE POSITION TO THE PERSON WHO WE LAST INTERVIEWED. TELL ME WHY I SHOULDN'T?

This question is very similar to the previous one but is a little bit more ruthless. Basically you need to sell yourself even more and be positive in your response.

Try to adapt the following response to your own individual attributes:

"Because I genuinely believe that I'm the best person for the job. I understand that there are other people who have the ability to do this job and are highly capable. But I know that I also have that ability. Along with that I bring additional qualities that make me the very best person for the job. My attitude and commitment towards achieving excellence are unparalleled. In my previous role I achieved excellence time and again. I also constantly look for ways to improve myself. To that end I have embarked on an educational course to improve my skills in XYZ. If I am successful today I promise I will impress you and will not let you down. If I am not successful then I will be applying for the next vacancy as I would love to work for your company."

Once again, use the template on the following page to create your own response. When creating your own response consider using the following powerful words:

- Ambitious
- Driven
- Hard-working
- Dedicated
- Flexible
- Adaptable
- Caring
- Considerate
- Professional

TEMPLATE FOR QUESTION 18 – I AM CONSIDERING
GIVING THE POSITION TO THE PERSON WHO WE LAST
INTERVIEWED. TELL ME WHY I SHOULDN'T?

QUESTION 19 – WHAT QUALITIES DO YOU BELIEVE A GOOD MANAGER SHOULD HAVE?

You are more likely to be asked this type of question if you are applying for a managerial position. If you are applying for a managerial or supervisory position then this question is designed to find out what you will be like as a manager. Managers are required to lead and also to be great role models for the organisation. Have a look at the following response and use it to structure your own answer using the template on the following page.

"The key quality should be leadership and the ability to look ahead towards the horizon. The manager needs to be ten steps ahead and already making plans for the future. They also should be good role models and be capable of leading by example. Approachable, fair and enthusiastic are other important qualities but above all a successful manager needs to lead when things aren't going as planned. It is his or her responsibility to lift a team out of a difficult period and motivate people to achieve the vision of the organisation. The highest calling of a true leader is inspiring others to reach the highest of their abilities. The company's aims, objectives and vision are what the manager should work towards and have at the forefront of his/her mind at all times."

Some of the qualities of a competent manager include:

- Being a visionary and a role model for the company
- Being able to delegate work effectively
- Identifying strengths in employees and using those strengths effectively
- Identifying development needs in individuals and providing appropriate feedback and support where necessary
- Being flexible and adaptable when required
- Being capable of implementing the company's policies, procedures and vision
- Leading by example

TEMPLATE FOR QUESTION 19 – WHAT QUALITIES DO YOU
BELIEVE A GOOD MANAGER SHOULD HAVE?

QUESTION 20 – CAN YOU TELL US ABOUT A SITUATION WHEN YOU HAVE HAD TO WORK UNDER PRESSURE?

Some jobs, such as sales and customer service roles, will require you to work under pressure. The interviewer will therefore want to know that you have the ability to perform in such an environment. If you have experience of working under pressure then you are far more likely to succeed in a high-pressurised role. When responding to a question of this nature, try to provide an actual example of where you have achieved a task whilst being under pressure.

There now follows a sample response to this question. Once you have read it, take the time to construct your own response based on your own individual experiences and knowledge using the template provided.

"Yes, I can. In my current job as car mechanic for a well-known company, I was presented with a difficult and pressurised situation. A member of the team had made a mistake and had fitted a number of wrong components to a car. The car in question was due to be picked up at 2pm and the customer had stated how important it was that his car was ready on time because he had an important meeting to attend. We only had two hours in which to resolve the issue and I volunteered to be the one who would carry out the work on the car. The problem was that we had three other customers in the workshop waiting for their cars too, so I was the only person who could be spared at that particular time. I worked solidly for the next two hours making sure that I meticulously carried out each task in line with our operating procedures. Even though I didn't finish the car until 2.10pm, I managed to achieve a very difficult task under pressurised conditions whilst keeping strictly to procedures and regulations."

TEMPLATE FOR QUESTION 20 – CAN YOU TELL US ABOUT
A SITUATION WHEN YOU HAVE HAD TO WORK UNDER
PRESSURE?

QUESTION 21 – CAN YOU TELL ME ABOUT A TIME WHEN YOU
HAVE WORKED AS PART OF A TEAM TO ACHIEVE A GOAL?

Having the ability to work as part of a team is very important to the vast
majority of jobs that you will apply for. Most large companies will employ
many people in many different roles ranging from customer service and
administration, through to management and operations. In fact it is not
uncommon for thousands of people to work for one particular company.
Therefore, it is essential that every member of the team works together in
order to achieve the ultimate goal that the company sets. The interviewer
will want to be certain that you can work effectively as part of a team,
which is why you may be asked questions that relate to your team working
experience during a job interview.

There now follows a sample response to this question. Once you have read
it, take time to construct your own response using the template provided.

*"Yes, I can. I like to keep fit and healthy and as part of this aim I play football
for a local Sunday team. We had worked very hard to get to the cup final
and we were faced with playing a very good opposition team who had
recently won the league title. After only ten minutes of play, one of our
players was sent off and we conceded a penalty as a result. Being one
goal down and with 80 minutes left to play, we were faced with a mountain
to climb. However, we all remembered our training and worked very hard
in order to prevent any more goals being scored. Due to playing with ten
players, I had to switch positions and play as a defender, something that I
am not used to. The team worked brilliantly to hold off any further opposing
goals and after 60 minutes we managed to get an equaliser. The game went
to penalties in the end and we managed to win the cup. I believe I am an
excellent team player and can always be relied upon to work as an effective
team member at all times."*

TEMPLATE FOR QUESTION 21 – CAN YOU TELL ME ABOUT
A TIME WHEN YOU HAVE WORKED AS PART OF A TEAM
TO ACHIEVE A GOAL?

QUESTION 22 – CAN YOU PROVIDE US WITH AN EXAMPLE OF A PROJECT YOU HAVE HAD TO COMPLETE AND THE OBSTACLES YOU HAD TO OVERCOME?

Having the ability to complete tasks and projects successfully demonstrates that you have the ability to persevere and complete tasks that will form part of your role. Many people give up on things in life and fail to achieve their goals. Any interviewer will want to be convinced that you are going to complete all on-the-job training successfully and, if you can provide evidence of where you have already done this, then this will go in your favour.

When responding to this type of question, try to think of a difficult, drawn out task that you achieved despite a number of obstacles that were in your way. You may choose to use examples from your work life or even from some recent academic work that you have carried out. Take a look at the following sample question before using the template provided to construct your own response based on your own experiences.

"Yes I can. I recently successfully completed a NEBOSH course (National Examination Board in Occupational Safety and Health) via distance learning. The course took two years to complete in total and I had to carry out all studying in my own time whilst holding down my current job.

The biggest obstacle I had to overcome was finding the time to complete the work to the high standard that I wanted to achieve. I decided to manage my time effectively and I allocated two hours every evening of the working week in which to complete the work required. I found the time management difficult but I stuck with it and I was determined to complete the course. In the end I achieved very good results and I very much enjoyed the experience and challenge. I have a determined nature and I have the ability to concentrate for long periods of time when required. I can be relied upon to finish projects to a high standard."

TEMPLATE FOR QUESTION 22 – CAN YOU PROVIDE
US WITH AN EXAMPLE OF A PROJECT YOU HAVE HAD
TO COMPLETE AND THE OBSTACLES YOU HAD TO
OVERCOME?

QUESTION 23 – WHAT IS YOUR SICKNESS RECORD LIKE AND WHAT DO YOU THINK IS AN ACCEPTABLE LEVEL OF SICKNESS?

Most employers detest sickness, and they especially detest sickness that is not genuine. For every day that an employee is off sick, it will cost the company dearly in both financial terms, and also in terms of productivity. Therefore, they want to employ people who have a good sickness record. Obviously you cannot lie when responding to this question, as the company you are applying to join will carry out checks and references.

The latter part of the question is simple to answer. Basically no amount of sickness is acceptable but sometimes genuine sickness cannot be avoided. Remember to tell the interviewer that you do not take time off sick unless absolutely necessary and you can be relied upon to come to work.

Take a look at the following sample response before using the template on the following page to create a response based on your own views and opinions.

"Any form of sickness is not acceptable. However, sometimes people need to go off sick if they are genuinely ill. I would always try my hardest to get into work. If I was ill then I would much prefer it if my line manager sent me home rather than calling in sick. Having said that, I would not want to give a cold or bug to other staff members in the office, as this could have an even worse effect on the company. During the last 12 months I have had only 4 days sickness. These days were for food poisoning, and there was no way I could get out of bed! I fully understand the importance of maintaining a good attendance record and I can always be relied upon not to go off sick unless I am genuinely ill. My previous employer will indicate this in any reference."

TEMPLATE FOR QUESTION 23 – WHAT IS YOUR SICKNESS RECORD LIKE AND WHAT DO YOU THINK IS AN ACCEPTABLE LEVEL OF SICKNESS?

QUESTION 24 – WHAT ARE THE MISSION AND AIMS OF THIS
COMPANY?

Many organisations set themselves aims and objectives. These are
sometimes in the form of a vision or charter. They usually relate to the high
level of customer service that they promise to deliver. When you apply
for any role you should not only prepare for each stage of the selection
process but you should also learn as much as possible about the company
you are applying to join. Learning this kind of information is important and
it will demonstrate your seriousness about joining their particular company.
Visit the website of the company you are applying for in order to view their
mission, aims, objectives or customer charter.

The following is a sample fictitious customer charter:

DELIVERING QUALITY SERVICE EVERY TIME

The Customer Charter sets out our commitment to delivering a
high standard of customer service. It outlines:

- the type of service we aim to provide
- how to contact us and give us feedback, particularly if
  anything goes wrong, and
- how you can assist us to better serve you

Our goal is to help you achieve what you need by providing quality
advice, products and services. We believe that excellent customer
relationships are the result of us working together to deliver great
outcomes for you by:

- developing trust through open, honest and simple
  communication
- being approachable and listening to your views
- treating you with fairness and respect
- ensuring ease, expertise and efficiency when you deal with us

---

Now use the template on the following page to create a response to this
question following your research into the company/organisation you are
applying to join.

TEMPLATE FOR QUESTION 24 – WHAT ARE THE MISSION
AND AIMS OF THIS COMPANY?

QUESTION 25 – ARE YOU WILLING TO RELOCATE?

This is a difficult question to answer. The interviewer would not normally ask this type of question unless there was a requirement to relocate now or in the future. If there is a potential requirement for you to relocate with the job that you are applying for and you answer the question negatively with a 'no', then there is a good chance that you will not get the job. Therefore, the most appropriate answer in this circumstance would be 'yes', providing that is you actually mean it! It is acceptable, however, to ask questions at the end of the interview about relocation packages or the time that you would be expected to relocate. Most of us do not want to relocate and therefore there should be an incentive for a move.

"Yes I would be willing to relocate and I have already discussed this with my family. Naturally I would like to discuss the relocation package that the company offers if I was to be successful, but I fully appreciate that there may be a need to relocate. If I ever achieved promotion within the company then I would certainly be willing to relocate. I am committed to this job longterm and would do everything within reason to work hard for the company and if that meant being in a different location then I would rise to the challenge. I have had plenty of experience moving around and I know that I could settle into a new environment quickly."

Use the template on the following page to create a response based on your own views and circumstances.

TEMPLATE FOR QUESTION 25 – ARE YOU WILLING TO RELOCATE?

QUESTION 26 – CAN YOU TELL US ABOUT A SITUATION WHERE YOU DEMONSTRATED LEADERSHIP?

Before we take a look at a sample response to this question, first we need to explore the definition of 'leadership'. A simple definition of leadership is that leadership is the art of motivating a group of people to act towards achieving a common goal. Put even more simply, the leader is the inspiration and director of the action. He or she is the person in the group that possesses the combination of personality and skills that makes others want to follow his or her direction. Ok, now that we understand what leadership means, here is a sample response:

"One evening, at the change of shift, I became aware that two members of the team were late for work. There had been heavy snowfall that day and the congestion on the surrounding roads meant that many people could not get to work. I took it upon myself to lead the team through the coming shift and, despite being two people down, we managed to achieve the goal of providing first class service to our customers. To begin with, I briefed the remainder of the team on the difficulty of the task that lay ahead of us. I assessed the skill levels and experience within the team and allocated tasks accordingly. I ensured that I remained confident and in control during the brief so that the team members would have confidence in my ability to manage the problem. As the shift progressed I had a number of different problems to deal with but I remained calm, listened carefully to the problems, and directed accordingly. At the end of the shift we congratulated ourselves on a job well done and discussed the areas in which we felt we could improve, if the same situation was to arise again."

Now use the template on the following page to create a response based on your own views and circumstances.

TEMPLATE FOR QUESTION 26 – CAN YOU TELL US ABOUT
A SITUATION WHERE YOU DEMONSTRATED LEADERSHIP?

QUESTION 27 – CAN YOU EXPLAIN THE DIFFERENCE BETWEEN A MANAGER AND A LEADER?

During my time as an Officer in the Fire Service I was required to both manage and lead teams of people. The difference between a manager and a leader can be summed up as follows:

It is a manager's responsibility to make effective use of the resources that are at his/her disposal. This may include planning ahead, ensuring there are sufficient resources available, and making the best use of their teams skills, strengths and qualities. A leader will use his or her skills and experiences to motivate the team and direct them towards the desired goal. All good leaders will be visionaries who have one eye on the end target.

KEYWORDS USED TO DESCRIBE THE FUNCTIONS OF A MANAGER

- Planning
- Effective use of resources
- Strategic thinking
- Organising

KEYWORDS USED TO DESCRIBE THE FUNCTIONS OF A LEADER

- Visionary
- Motivator
- Inspiring

If you can provide specific examples in your response where you have demonstrated leadership skills and also management skills then even better!

QUESTION 28 – WHAT MAKES A GOOD LEADER?

In order to become a good leader you must have a number of different skills that you can draw upon at a moment's notice and these include:

Being a visionary – An ability to see the end result or the desired goal.

Provide inspiration – Great leaders need to be capable of inspiring their team towards a goal or objective.

Strategic thinker – Being able to think outside of the box and plan for the future.

Being liked by the team – Whilst not essential, it certainly helps to be liked by your team. If they like you, the will follow you.

Being an effective decision maker – Having the ability to make decisions, even sometimes unpopular ones.

Accepting of feedback and criticism – Good leaders should be able to take criticism from others. This will help them to continually improve.

Whilst the above list is not exhaustive, it will provide you with a number of useful tips that will assist you during your preparation.

QUESTION 29 – WHAT HAS BEEN YOUR BIGGEST FAILURE TO DATE?

Now this really is a difficult question to answer! Get this wrong and it could be all over. The majority of people will answer this question in the following manner:

"To be honest, I don't normally fail at anything. I prepare so well for everything that I do that success is inevitable."

Well, if you answer it in this style then you are probably about to just fail your first big thing – your interview!

Everybody makes mistakes. Everybody fails at something. It's what you do about the failure that's the important part. Take a look at the following sample response:

"I would say my biggest failure to date is failing an educational course that I embarked upon approximately two years ago. The reason why I failed the course was primarily due to a lack of adequate time set aside for studying. However, I immediately learnt from my mistakes and shortcomings and I booked to re-sit the test immediately. I worked hard during the build up to the re-sit and I spent lots of time studying. I passed the test with flying colours. I certainly learnt a lot from my initial failure and I always make sure that I now prepare fully for everything that I do."

Now use the template on the following page to create a response based on your own failures and lessons learnt.

TEMPLATE FOR QUESTION 29 – WHAT HAS BEEN YOUR
BIGGEST FAILURE TO DATE?

QUESTION 30 – DO YOU NEED OTHER PEOPLE AROUND TO STIMULATE YOU, OR ARE YOU SELF-MOTIVATED?

Most employers want their staff to be self-motivated. If an employee is self-motivated then he or she are going to perform to a high standard. Having personally employed people in the past, I find that those individuals who are self-motivated will do a good job for me. They will find things to do when it is quiet, and they will also be motivated by their own success and achievements at work. Whilst pay is a motivating factor for an employee, it is not the most important. Job satisfaction is vital if a person is going to perform well at work.

Your response to this question should focus on providing examples of where you have been self-motivated in a current or previous work role. It is easy for an interviewee to say that they are self-motivated, but proving it with examples is a different matter.

Take a look at the following sample response:

"Whilst I enjoy working in a team environment I am a highly self-motivated person. I don't like it when I'm sat around doing nothing, so I'm always on the look out for new things to do. That applies to when I'm either at home or at work. For example, during my last job when we were going through a quiet spell, I wanted to look for ways to improve the company turnover. Without being asked I set about researching different areas that the company could potentially draw more income streams from. I contacted a number of potential customers and arranged to send them some company literature and sample products. From this work I managed to created six new leads for the company and my manager was very pleased with the fact that I'd been self-motivated enough to try to make a positive difference."

Now use the template on the following page to create a response based on your own experiences.

TEMPLATE FOR QUESTION 30 – DO YOU NEED OTHER PEOPLE AROUND TO STIMULATE YOU, OR ARE YOU SELF-MOTIVATED?

QUESTION 31 – ARE YOU ACCEPTED INTO A TEAM QUICKLY?

Remember that teamwork is very important in the vast majority of organisations. Therefore, being able to fit into a team environment will be a positive thing. Again, I would advise that you try to think of examples where you have previously joined a new team, and adapted quickly.

Take a look at the following sample response:

"I am inherently a great team player, so the answer to this question would have to be a definite yes. I have worked in lots or teams in the past and this is usually when I am at my best. I understand that when you join a new team you need to fit into the new environment and make an effort to introduce yourself, get to know the people in the team and also how the team operates. I believe that, by understanding the key elements of a team, I am capable of quickly being accepted in the vast majority of teams. Team members need to be good communicators, listeners, supporters and motivators. Each team needs a variety of different skill-sets and I believe I have lots of qualities to bring to any team environment.

Whilst working for a previous employer I was required to join a new team because a lady had gone on maternity leave. I quickly assessed the dynamics of the team and tried to fit in as best that I could. Because I was so adaptable, each member of the team welcomed me and helped me to get settled in quickly. I understand that if I am successful then I will be required to quickly adapt to the team environment. This will not be a problem for me and I am in fact looking forward to the new challenge."

Once again, use the template on the following page to create a response based on your own experiences.

TEMPLATE FOR QUESTION 31 – ARE YOU ACCEPTED INTO A TEAM QUICKLY?

QUESTION 32 – CAN YOU RUN A MEETING, AND IF SO, HOW WOULD YOU DO IT?

Having personally chaired many meetings during my career, I have learnt to realise that the person who is tasked with the responsibility of chairing the meeting must ensure they maintain control over proceedings. If they don't, then the meeting can quickly become a waste of time.

If you have any experience of running meetings then this will obviously be an advantage if you are required to respond to a question of this nature. If you haven't, then take a look at the following response for some great ideas on how to successfully run a meeting:

"Yes I do have some experience of running meetings. To begin with, I would plan thoroughly for the meeting. This would usually be done at least the day before, if not sooner. I would ensure that the meeting room was booked and that any relevant features were available, such as presentation aids. I would make sure that everyone was notified of the meeting date, time and venue, and provide them with an agenda. I would make notes prior to the meeting and also set a timeframe in which I would want the meeting to conclude. I am aware that meetings can sometimes drag. I would be keen to avoid any irrelevant discussions and keep the meeting focused on the agenda items. If the meeting was starting to slip, then I would be keen to bring it back in line with the programme. I would make sure that everybody had the opportunity to speak during the meeting and would provide a note taker so that all of the salient points could be documented. Once the meeting was over I would make sure that everyone received a copy of the minutes and more importantly the matters arising from the meetings."

Now use the template on the following page to create a response based on your own experiences and how you would run a meeting if required.

TEMPLATE FOR QUESTION 32 – CAN YOU RUN A MEETING,
AND IF SO, HOW WOULD YOU DO IT?

QUESTION 33 – WHAT DO YOU THINK THE QUALITIES OF A GOOD TEAM PLAYER ARE?

Having knowledge of how a team operates and the qualities required to become a competent team player would be an advantage before you attend your interview. Take a look at the following 'team' qualities:

- An ability to interact and work with others, regardless of their age, sex, religion, sexual orientation, background, disability or appearance;
- Being able to communicate with everyone in the team and provide the appropriate level of support and encouragement;
- Being capable of carrying out tasks correctly, professionally and in accordance with guidelines and regulations;
- Being focused on the team's goal(s);
- Having a flexible attitude and approach to the task;
- Putting the needs of the team first before your own;
- Putting personal differences aside for the sake of the team;
- Being able to listen to others' suggestions and contributions.

When responding to this type of question it would be an advantage if you could back up your response with an example of where you have already work in a team. Take a look at the following sample response:

"A good team player must have many different qualities including an ability to listen carefully to a given brief. If you don't listen to the brief that is provided then you can't complete the task properly. In addition to listening carefully to the brief you must be able to communicate effectively with everyone in the team. This will include providing support for the other team members and also listening to other people's suggestions on how a task can be achieved. You also have to be able to work with anyone in the team regardless of their age, background, religion, sexual orientation, disability or appearance. You can't discriminate against anyone and if you do, then there is no place for you within that team. A good team player must also be able to carry out his or her job professionally and competently. When I say competently I mean correctly and in accordance with guidelines and training. You should also be focused on the team's goal and not be distracted by any external factors. Putting the needs of the team first is paramount. Finally a good team player must be flexible and be able to adapt to the changing requirements of the team.

I already have some experience of working in a team and I know how important it is to work hard at achieving the task. In a previous job we would have a weekly team briefing. During the team briefings my manager would inform us what jobs need to be carried out as a priority. During one particular meeting he asked three of us to clear a fire escape that had become blocked with cardboard boxes, debris and rubbish. He also asked us to come up with a plan to prevent it from happening again. We quickly set about the task carefully removing the rubbish and I had the responsibility of arranging for a refuse collection company to come and dispose of the rubbish. We also had to work together to find ways of preventing the rubbish from being haphazardly disposed in the same way again in the future. We sat down together and wrote out a memorandum for our manager that he could distribute to all staff. At the end of the job we'd worked well to achieve the task and no more rubbish was ever disposed in the fire escape again. My manager was very pleased with the job we'd done."

Now use the template on the following page to create a response based on your own skills and experiences.

TEMPLATE FOR QUESTION 33 – WHAT DO YOU THINK THE
QUALITIES OF A GOOD TEAM PLAYER ARE?

QUESTION 34 – CAN YOU TELL ME ABOUT ANY ACHIEVEMENTS YOU HAVE EXPERIENCED DURING YOUR LIFE SO FAR?

Those people who can demonstrate a history of achievement are far more likely to continue to succeed in their new working environment. Having achieved something in your life demonstrates that you have the ability to see things through to the end, something that is crucial to your new career. It also shows that you are motivated and determined to succeed. Try to think of examples where you have succeeded or achieved something relevant in your life. Some good examples of achievements are as follows:

- Winning a trophy with a football or hockey team;
- GCSEs and other educational qualifications;
- Duke of Edinburgh's Award;
- Being given responsibility at work or at school;
- Raising money for charity.

"Yes I can. So far in my life I have achieved quite a few things that I am proud of. To begin with I achieved good grades whilst at school including a grade 'A' in English. I worked very hard to achieve my grades and I'm proud of them. At weekends I play rugby for a local team and I've achieved a number of things with them. Apart from winning the league last year we also held a charity match against the local Police rugby team. We managed to raise £500 for a local charity, which was a great achievement. More recently I managed to achieve a huge increase in my fitness levels. I have learnt that you have to work hard in life if you want to achieve things and I have a positive attitude to hard work. My own personal motto is 'work hard and you'll be rewarded'."

Now use the template on the following page to create a response based on your own skills and experiences.

TEMPLATE FOR QUESTION 34 – CAN YOU TELL ME ABOUT
ANY ACHIEVEMENTS YOU HAVE EXPERIENCED DURING
YOUR LIFE SO FAR?

QUESTION 35 – WHAT IS THE BEST EXAMPLE OF CUSTOMER SERVICE YOU HAVE COME ACROSS?

This type of question is designed to see how high your standards are, in relation to customer service. Try to think of an occasion when you have witnessed an excellent piece of customer service and show that you learned from it. If you are very confident, then you may have an occasion when you, yourself, provided that service. Whatever response you provide, make sure it is unique and stands out.

"Whilst working as a shop assistant in my current role, a member of the public came in to complain to the manager about a pair of football shoes that he had bought for his son's birthday. When his son came to open the present on the morning of his birthday, he noticed that one of the football boots was a larger size than the other. He was supposed to be playing football with his friends that morning and wanted to wear his new boots. However, due to the shop's mistake, this was not possible. Naturally, the boy was very upset. The manager of the shop was excellent in her approach to dealing with situation. She remained calm throughout and listened to the gentleman very carefully, showing complete empathy for his son's situation. This immediately diffused any potential confrontation. She then told him how sorry she was for the mistake that had happened, and that she would feel exactly the same if it was her own son who it had happened to. She then told the gentleman that she would refund the money in full and give his son a new pair of football boots to the same value as the previous pair. The man was delighted with her offer. Not only that, she then offered to give the man a further discount of 10% on any future purchase, due to the added inconvenience that was caused by him having to return to the shop to sort out the problem. I learned a lot from the way my manager dealt with this situation. She used exceptional communication skills and remained calm throughout. She then went the extra mile to make the gentleman's journey back to the shop a worthwhile one. The potential for losing a customer was averted by her actions and I felt sure the man would return to our shop again."

TEMPLATE FOR QUESTION 35 – WHAT IS THE BEST
EXAMPLE OF CUSTOMER SERVICE YOU HAVE COME
ACROSS?

QUESTION 36 – HOW WOULD YOU DEAL WITH SOMEBODY IN A WORK SITUATION WHO YOU FELT WAS NOT PULLING THEIR WEIGHT OR WORKING AS PART OF THE TEAM?

This question is primarily designed at assessing your assertiveness and confidence, whilst also being tactful. The interview panel are not looking for you to respond in a confrontational manner but, instead, they are looking for you to approach the person and resolve the issue in an amicable manner. To ignore the issue is not an option.

Take a look at the following sample response:

"Whilst working in my current role as a waiter for a local restaurant, I was aware of a colleague who was taking more breaks than he was entitled to. Whilst he was taking these additional breaks, the rest of the team would have to cover for the shortfall. Unfortunately, the customer would then suffer, as the time it took for them to be served would increase. I decided to approach the person in order to resolve the issue. I walked over to him and asked him in a friendly manner if he would come and help the rest of team serve the customers. I told him that we were busy and that we needed his help. Fortunately, he responded in a positive manner and realised that he was taking advantage of his rest periods. Since then, there has not been an issue. It is important that the team gets on and works well together. We cannot afford to have confrontational situations and the best way to resolve issues like this is to be honest and tactful."

Now use the template on the following page to create a response based on your own skills and experiences.

TEMPLATE FOR QUESTION 36 – HOW WOULD YOU DEAL
WITH SOMEBODY IN A WORK SITUATION WHO YOU FELT
WAS NOT PULLING THEIR WEIGHT OR WORKING AS PART
OF THE TEAM?

QUESTION 37 – WHAT DO YOU DISLIKE DOING IN A WORK ENVIRONMENT?

Be very careful how you respond to this type of question. The things that you dislike should be totally disassociated with any elements of the job you are applying for. For example, if you are applying for a job that is primarily customer-focused, don't tell the panel that you dislike dealing with people's problems or queries. If you are applying for an office job, don't tell the panel that you dislike being sat behind a desk all day. You should also avoid responses that portray yourself as a person who is not self-motivated. I can remember asking this question to an applicant during an interview and he replied with:

"I don't like having nothing to do. I get bored if there's not much to do in the office. I enjoy being busy at work and I like to be kept active."

On the face of it, this doesn't appear to be a bad response. However, a person who is sat around doing nothing should be looking for other things to do whilst at work. There are always things to do in a working environment, whether that's organising the following days work, or even asking fellow colleagues if they need help with any element of their own work.

"There's nothing in particular that I dislike doing in a working environment. Whilst I like to be kept active, if I have completed all of my work for the day, then I will always look for other things to do, or even offer to help a work colleague with their work. Sometimes at work we have to carry out monotonous and repetitive tasks. Whilst these aren't my favourite parts of the working day, I always carry them out diligently and professionally."

Now use the template on the following page to create a response based on your views and opinions.

TEMPLATE FOR QUESTION 37 – WHAT DO YOU DISLIKE
DOING IN A WORK ENVIRONMENT?

QUESTION 38 – HOW WOULD YOU FEEL ABOUT WORKING FOR SOMEONE WHO IS YOUNGER THAN YOURSELF, OR OF THE OPPOSITE SEX?

This question is obviously designed to assess whether you are ageist or sexist. Some people do have a problem with working for someone who is younger than them. Trust me, I know! When I was in the Fire Service I was promoted to a Sub Officer at a very young age. I was in charge of a watch that had 18 people on it. There was one man in particular who took immediate dislike to working under someone who was 20 years his junior. Whilst this didn't faze me, it was clearly a problem for him. In the modern day working environment you must feel comfortable with working for people who are either younger than yourself, or of the opposite sex. I have had the pleasure of working for some fantastic female bosses who were also a lot younger than me. I would always do everything I could to support a manager and carry out my job competently and professionally, and so should you.

"I am of the clear opinion that it doesn't matter what sex you are, or what age you are; you can still have a tremendous amount to offer a team or a company. I would have absolutely no problem with working for anyone who was younger, older or of the opposite sex to me. In a previous job, where I had been working for eight years, a female work colleague got the promotion that we had both been going for. She was ten years younger than me and had only been with the company for six months. She was clearly a very talented person; I was the first to congratulate her and informed her that I would support her fully in her new role. Over the forthcoming twelve months we built up a fantastic working relationship and I learnt a lot from her professionally. The team was really buzzing and I have to say it was probably my most enjoyable twelve months with that company whilst working for her."

Now use the template on the following page to create a response based on your views and opinions.

TEMPLATE FOR QUESTION 38 – HOW WOULD YOU FEEL
ABOUT WORKING FOR SOMEONE WHO IS YOUNGER
THAN YOURSELF, OR OF THE OPPOSITE SEX?

QUESTION 39 – WHAT SALARY ARE YOU LOOKING FOR?

This can be a very tricky question to answer. Everybody wants to earn the highest salary possible; yet at the same time you do not want to come across as either arrogant or overconfident. The key to answering this question is to make sure you justify the salary that you are after.

Personally, when responding to this question, I will always go for the highest salary possible. I do this with the thinking that I can always come down a little if they decide that they don't want to pay me what I believe I am worth. Remember that you only get one chance to provide a figure. If that figure is low, then there's no way that you'll be able to negotiate an increased amount. Be confident and be comfortable with the amount that you want.

Sample response based on a wage band of £17,000 – £24,000

"I would like a salary of £23,500 per annum. The reason why I would like this amount is simply because I have the skills, qualifications and experience to perform exceptionally in the role. Even though I believe I am worth £24,000, I would much prefer to start on a lower scale and prove to you how good I am. I feel very strongly that you'll be pleased with my performance and that I am worth this salary. Although money is not the main motivating factor for me, I do believe that I am worth this amount."

The above sample response displays a level of confidence that the employer will find appealing. However, if you say you are good at a job, then you will need to prove this during your initial probationary period.

Now use the template on the following page to create a response based on your skills, qualifications and experiences.

TEMPLATE FOR QUESTION 39 – WHAT SALARY ARE YOU
LOOKING FOR?

QUESTION 40 – WHAT DIDN'T YOU LIKE ABOUT YOUR LAST JOB?

If you are applying to move jobs into an external company then there will obviously be a reason why you want to move. We all have bad experiences in the working environment, and more often than not, the majority of people want to move simply because that either don't like their boss, or the people that they work with. Whatever you do, do not be disrespectful to any of your previous managers or work colleagues, no matter how much you disliked them! You should also avoid using salary as a motivating factor for moving jobs. I have heard some horror responses to this question during my time as an interviewer. Here's one of them:

"To be honest, I don't get on well with my boss. He treats me poorly and everyone in the office thinks he's a bully."

Whilst I didn't doubt the person's claims, I believe that any grievances should be kept to yourself. The key to answering this question successfully is to choose a genuine reason that shows you are motivated, and also that you want a new and fresh challenge.

"Basically I am ready for a new challenge. I have been in my previous role for seven years now and I feel the time has come for me to move on. I get on very well with my manager and all of the members in my team. Whilst I will miss them, I don't feel that I can develop any further in the same position. I am applying for this new job, as I believe I can offer a great deal in terms of my skills and experiences. I am really looking forward to a new challenge and the benefits of working in a brand new environment."

Now use the template on the following page to create a response based on your reasons for moving jobs.

TEMPLATE FOR QUESTION 40 – WHAT DIDN'T YOU LIKE
ABOUT YOUR LAST JOB?

QUESTION 41 – WE THINK THAT YOU MIGHT BE OVERQUALIFIED FOR THIS JOB. WHAT DO YOU THINK?

This question will only ever be asked if you really are overqualified for the position. Whilst the question is somewhat flattering, you need to answer in a manner that displaces any element of doubt amongst the interview panel. The reason why an interviewer would ask this question is simply because they do not want you to become bored quickly with the post, and then move on to another position with another company. You need to prove within your response that the position you are applying for is not just a stopgap.

"Whilst I admit I am very well qualified, I don't personally believe that I am overqualified for this post. I am the type of person who does not become bored easily, simply because I am always being creative and looking for new things to do in the workplace. I believe I can be a valuable asset in this post and the extra skills that I do have will hopefully be shared amongst the team. There are many jobs that I could have applied for, but I chose this one because I want to work for your company and your team. It has a very good reputation and everyone who I have spoken to during my research is very satisfied in their job. I have spent much of my career learning new skills and gaining qualifications. Whilst I am always willing to take on new challenges, I am looking for a more stable job where I am comfortable in the role. I can assure you that I will not become bored easily and that whilst I am very well qualified, this will not be an issue. If I am successful then I would like to stay in the post for a long time."

Now use the template on the following page to create a response based on your skills, experiences and qualifications.

TEMPLATE FOR QUESTION 41 – WE THINK THAT YOU
MIGHT BE OVERQUALIFIED FOR THIS JOB. WHAT DO YOU
THINK?

QUESTION 42 – WE PRESUME THAT YOU HAVE READ THE JOB DESCRIPTION, SO THEREFORE WHICH AREAS OF THE JOB APPEAL TO YOU THE LEAST?

During an earlier section of this guide I explained how important it is to read and study the job description and person specification for the job. This question is one of the reasons why you must do just that! If you don't know what is contained within these important documents, then not only should you not be applying for the job, you'll also have no hope of answering the question.

Most interviewers will assess you against the job description. The job description is basically a blueprint for the role that you are applying for and it determines the skills and attributes required to perform the job competently. Make sure you read the job description and also have examples ready of where you match each assessable area.

"Yes I have been studying the job description for some time now. To be honest, there aren't any elements that I wouldn't find appealing. To begin with, the requirement to deal with customers' queries and complaints is something that I would very much enjoy. I get a lot of satisfaction out of helping people so this would not be a problem for me. The part in the description that requires you to respond quickly to queries, again is not an issue. I am very organised and always complete tasks at the soonest opportunity. I also understand that there is a requirement for me to record details of every telephone call that I handle. This is fundamental to the role as it is important to keep a track of progress when dealing with customers' issues. Again, this would not be a problem for me simply because I enjoy being organised. As mentioned already, there are no elements of the job description that I would dislike. I have carefully studied all elements and would relish the opportunity to work in this role."

Now use the template on the following page to create a response based on your research of the job description for the role you are applying for.

TEMPLATE FOR QUESTION 42 – WE PRESUME THAT YOU
HAVE READ THE JOB DESCRIPTION, SO THEREFORE
WHICH AREAS OF THE JOB APPEAL TO YOU THE LEAST?

QUESTION 43 – HERE'S A PEN; SELL IT TO ME!

This type of question will only normally be asked during interviews for sales roles.

It is designed to assess your selling ability. Of course, a pen is just a pen; a piece of plastic containing some ink and a roller ball. However, the pen has significant benefits and advantages for the user, and this is how you should pitch your response to this question – focusing on the benefits and advantages to the user.

Take a look at the following response:

"I'd like to introduce you to one of the world's greatest inventions – the pen. On first inspection, this small, perfectly formed implement does not appear to be capable of doing much. However, with just a small movement this pen has boundless creativity and it will allow you to communicate with whoever you wish, without having to say a single word vocally. Having personally been an owner of hundreds of pens during my working career, I am a true fan of this writing tool and can personally guarantee that you too will benefit from its truly amazing abilities. The roller ball is really smooth and gives excellent presentation. It is leak proof and slim and sits discretely in your pocket."

Even if you are not applying for a sales position, try creating your own individual response to this question using the template on the following page. Remember to create a response that focuses on the benefits of the pen and the advantages it has to the potential user.

TEMPLATE FOR QUESTION 43 – HERE'S A PEN; SELL IT TO ME!

QUESTION 44 – WHAT DO YOU THINK OF YOUR CURRENT COMPANY?

This question is common during interviews of all types. Whilst it is primarily aimed at assessing the reasons why you are wishing to leave your current employer, it also assesses how mature and professional you are as an employee. Regardless of what you truly think about your current employer, never be critical of them to others, especially during an interview. If you are critical of your previous employer during the interview, then there is strong chance that you could be critical of this new employer once you have started! Remember to always be professional during your responses to interview questions and never respond to questions based on your personal feelings.

The key to responding to this question correctly is to state that your previous employer gave you many different skills that would be of benefit to your potential new employer. Your current employer's loss if your next employer's gain.

"I think they are great. I've had a wonderful time with them over the last few years. They have been very supportive of me and helped me to develop both personally and professionally. They are a well-respected employer and I believe that the skills I have learnt from them will benefit me, and also the next organisation that I work for, which will hopefully be yours. Even though I have had a great time working for them, I am personally ready for a new challenge, which is why I am here today."

Now use the template on the following page to create a response based on your views and opinions of your current or previous employer.

TEMPLATE FOR QUESTION 44 – WHAT DO YOU THINK OF
YOUR CURRENT COMPANY?

QUESTION 45 – WE SEE HERE THAT YOU HAVE ONLY BEEN WITH YOUR CURRENT EMPLOYER FOR SIX MONTHS. WHY DO YOU WANT TO MOVE SO SOON?

This again is quite a tricky question to answer. I have looked at a person's CV and application form before they come into interview, and have often wondered why they want to move jobs so soon after joining. In order to convince me they need to have a very good response to this question.

Of course, the probable reason why someone wants to move so soon is because they are unhappy in their job. If this is really the case, then I would much rather if the person was honest. Take a look at the following response, which was very similar to a person's response after I had asked this exact question:

"I have to be honest here; the job that I joined isn't what I expected. Whilst the employer is very good, the job has turned out to be different than the one advertised. I applied to become a sales representative, which is where my strengths are, but the job has ended up being an office-based role that requires me to primarily deal with customer queries. Whilst I don't mind doing this, it isn't the job that I applied for or the one that was sold to me when I applied. I could sit here and give you other reasons why I want to move on so quickly, but it is important that I am honest. I want you to know that I am not the kind or person who jumps from job to job and I feel certain that my current employer will give me a glowing reference. I am looking for a stable job that is suited to my skills and experiences, and the one I am applying for today certainly fits that description perfectly."

Now use the template on the following page to create a response based on how you would respond to this question.

TEMPLATE FOR QUESTION 45 – WE SEE HERE THAT YOU
HAVE ONLY BEEN WITH YOUR CURRENT EMPLOYER FOR
SIX MONTHS. WHY DO YOU WANT TO MOVE SO SOON?

QUESTION 46 – WE SEE THERE HAVE BEEN SOME GAPS IN YOUR EMPLOYMENT. CAN YOU EXPLAIN THESE?

If you have had any gaps in your employment then it is advisable that you have a valid reason for them. When responding to this type of question try to provide beneficial reasons for the gaps. Some good reasons for gaps in employment might be:

- Taking time off work to complete a study of development course
- Travelling to develop yourself or learn about a different language or culture
- Helping sick relatives or friends
- Carrying out voluntary work or community work

However, some not so good reasons for gaps in employment are:

- Getting over a previous stressful job
- Going on holiday with your friends
- You fancied a break from employment all together

The above will most probably put off a potential employer as there is a strong chance that you might want to leave them for a further gap in your employment.

"I took six months out from work to concentrate on finishing my Diploma educational course. I was eager to gain good grades so I decided to take a gap in my employment to fulfill this desire. It turned out to be a very good choice as I achieved excellent grades."

Now use the template on the following page to create your own response to this question.

TEMPLATE FOR QUESTION 46 – WE SEE THERE HAVE
BEEN SOME GAPS IN YOUR EMPLOYMENT. CAN YOU
EXPLAIN THESE?

QUESTION 47 – HOW DO YOU DEFINE SUCCESS?

This question is design to assess what level of ambition you have. There is a great answer to this question. Here it is:

"I define success in a number of ways. In the working environment I define it as excelling in my position and achieving far more than is expected of me. For example, in my previous role I was required to achieve sales targets of at least a 15% increase on the previous year. I actually managed to achieve a 35% increase, which to me is a huge success. I also define success as being part of a great working team, where everyone is working in harmony towards achieving the company goal. I also define success as being able to achieve all of the targets and objectives within my annual appraisal. Every year so far I have managed to achieve this and I am very proud of my work rate to date.

Success for me is also about continuing improvement. I always have something on the go that I am working for. For example, I have just completed a sales management course where I learnt how to manage sales teams with a view to getting the most out of them.

On a personal level, success to me is keeping fit and healthy, and also having my friends and family around me. I am a stable and grounded person at home and this allows me to concentrate fully on my work when required."

When responding to this question do not be afraid of blowing your trumpet and making yourself look good. If you are a good employee, then make sure you tell them so. Try to show a good level of ambition, and if you can back it up with evidence of previous success, then even better!

Now use the template to create your own response to this question.

TEMPLATE FOR QUESTION 47 – HOW DO YOU DEFINE SUCCESS?

QUESTION 48 – WHERE DO YOU SEE YOURSELF IN 5 YEARS' TIME?

This question should be answered positively and with a degree of ambition. However, the degree of ambition will very much depend on the role that you are applying for. Some employers like to see a consistent turnover of staff, whilst others are looking for a more stable workforce.

Probably the worst response I have heard to this question was when a candidate replied with:

"I want to be sat in your seat."

Whilst part of me admired his enthusiasm, the other part didn't like his arrogance!

Take a look at the following response, which will give you a good indication as to how to approach this type of question.

"I am certainly an ambitious person and would hopefully have progressed within the company by that point. However, the most important thing for me is to learn my job properly and become competent in the role. It is also important for me to gain the respect of the other members of my team. Yes, I would like to move on within the company at some point but my priority is the job that I am applying for. In terms of development, I aim to have completed a number of internal training courses by the time 5 years is up. I want to be extremely good at my job and I want my employer to think that they have made the right choice in taking me on."

Now use the template on the following page to create your own response to this question.

TEMPLATE FOR QUESTION 48 – WHERE DO YOU SEE
YOURSELF IN 5 YEARS' TIME?

QUESTION 49 – WHAT ARE THE MAIN ISSUES FACING OUR INDUSTRY TODAY?

Having knowledge of the industry that you applying to join would certainly be an advantage before attending interview. This is especially the case when applying for management or supervisory roles. Let's assume that I am applying for a job in the retail sector today. During my preparation I would probably research websites such as www.retail-week.com. This would give me an unbiased view on the issues that are affecting this sector at this particular moment in time.

Take a look at the following response, which is based on somebody applying to join a retail company.

"At the current time many retailers are facing difficult trading conditions. There are a number of High Street chains closing branches as a result of the recent recession. However, some retailers including yours have managed to buck the trend and have seen positive growth patterns. This is due to innovative thinking and an ability to foresee changes in the market. Other issues that face this industry at present include the dilemma of whether or not to move more business across to the internet. The internet has seen significant growth of late and has been a positive source of income for many retailers. I believe the key to maintaining good growth and development within this industry rests with the managers and the staff that the company employs. Innovative and hard-working individuals will help a company move forward and continue to make significant profits despite the tough trading conditions."

Now use the template on the following page to create your own response to this question.

TEMPLATE FOR QUESTION 49 – WHAT ARE THE MAIN
ISSUES FACING OUR INDUSTRY TODAY?

QUESTION 50 – DO YOU HAVE ANY FINAL QUESTIONS FOR THE PANEL?

You've reached the end of the interview and the panel will now ask you a question similar to the above. How do you answer it without ruining your chances of success? I have seen people ruin their interview, simply by asking irrelevant and arrogant questions at the end. Be careful what you ask the panel and, if you do decide to ask questions, keep them to a minimum or two or three and ask questions that the panel can easily answer.

Take a look at the following sample responses:

"Yes I just have one question please. If I am to be successful, how soon would it be before I start?" This displays a level of enthusiasm.

"I noticed on your website that you have been running a campaign aimed at attracting more customers to your website. Has this been a success?" This displays an enthusiastic interest in their company and the fact that you have carried out some research.

"I appreciate that I am yet to find out whether or not I am successful, but is there anything I can read to prepare myself for the job, just in case I am successful?" This displays motivation and conscientiousness.

"I notice that you have introduced a new exciting product range. Has this been a success?" This displays an enthusiastic interest in their company and the fact that you have carried out some research.

Now use the template on the following page to create your own response to this question.

TEMPLATE FOR QUESTION 50 – DO YOU HAVE ANY FINAL
QUESTIONS FOR THE PANEL?

PROBING QUESTIONS

Probing questions are questions that follow on from initial interview questions. Let's take a look at a sample interview question:

Q. Can you give me an example of where you have carried out excellent customer service?

You reply with:

"Yes I can give you a number of different examples. One in particular involved an angry customer who wanted to complain about the poor level of service that he had received from a member of our sales team. I quickly calmed him down and listened very carefully to his complaint. I then did everything in my power to apologise and also to make things right for him. I then followed up the complaint with a telephone call ten days after to see if he was still satisfied with the way that I had handled his complaint. He was more than happy with the way that I dealt with his situation and thanked me for the great service."

The interview panel could ask many different types of probing question based on your response. Here are a few examples:

"How did you initially feel when the customer spoke to you in an angry manner?"

"What did you do exactly to make sure his complaint was dealt with effectively?"

"What particular skills did you use to diffuse the initial anger and confrontation?"

"What did you learn from this situation and would you do anything different next time?"

Probing questions are very difficult to predict, simply because the type that you will have to answer will very much depend on the responses that you provide to the questions. The key is to be prepared for them!

CHAPTER 4:
OVERCOMING INTERVIEW NERVES

Many people who have an interview coming up will get nervous. Some people will unfortunately experience uncontrollable nerves. It is only natural to feel nervous before an interview, but there are a number of things that you can do to get over these nerves. To begin with, lets take a look at a few of the more common pre-interview anxieties:

- Feeling generally nervous and anxious
- Sweaty hands and palms
- Trembling voice
- Sore head
- Aching muscles
- Dry mouth
- Increased heart beat
- Shaky hands

I can remember taking my driving test at the age of 17 and feeling a few of the above symptoms. In the build up to the test I had worried myself so much that eventually I thought, "What's the point in all of this? It's only a driving test, who cares if I fail?" I had seriously reached the point where I didn't really care anymore whether I passed or failed. Now this is probably going to sound stupid, but this change in attitude actually worked in my favour. I performed a lot better during the driving test, simply because inside I had stopped caring, and therefore the nerves went out of the window. Now I am not saying that you shouldn't care about your interview, because that would be silly. But what I am saying is that you can only do so much research and you can only do so many mock interviews. Once you have done sufficient preparation for the interview, and you will know when that time has come, then it is pointless worrying anymore about it. Do your research, do your preparation, and then go into the interview feeling free, calm and relaxed, and trust me, you will perform a whole lot better!

MOCK INTERVIEWS

Before I attend any interview I will always carry out a few mock interviews. This basically involves getting friend or relative to sit down and ask me the anticipated interview questions under formal conditions. In fact, I even put on my suit during the mock interview to make it as realistic as possible. I have found over the years that this approach works extremely well in allowing me to improve my confidence, so make sure you try it!

VISUALISING THE INTERVIEW BEFORE YOU ATTEND IT

This is a great method that works for many people. Before you attend the interview, try and visualise the entire process. Sit down in your favourite armchair and close your eyes. Think about driving to the interview with plenty of time to spare. You arrive early at the interview venue and sit in the car park composing yourself and reading the job description. When you walk into the interview room you are standing tall, smiling and feeling relaxed and confident. You introduce yourself in a polite manner and shake the hands of each panel member. They immediately warm to you and your responses to the questions are both positive and inspiring. At the end of the interview you feel confident that you have done your absolute best and there is a strong possibility that you will be successful.

The above method is a fantastic way of focusing yourself prior to any interview. If you try to visualise the entire process being successful before the event starts, then this will put you in the correct frame of mind.

CHAPTER 5:
THE COMMON INTERVIEW MISTAKES

NOT TAKING THE INTERVIEW SERIOUSLY

Too many people become complacent. Especially if they think the job is theirs, or should be theirs. There have been many examples where people walk into an interview with a cavalier attitude and end up not getting the job. Don't make the same mistake – whether you are confident you'll get the job or not, make sure you put in the same amount of preparation.

DRESSING DOWN

How you present yourself during an interview or even an initial meeting is very important. Even if you know that the firm allows its employees to dress down, don't ruin your chances of success by doing the same. Remember that you only get one chance to make a first impression.

FAILING TO DEMONSTRATE TO THE INTERVIEW PANEL THAT YOU ARE THE PERSON FOR THE JOB

Be familiar with the job description for the position you're being interviewed for so you can illustrate how your experience, abilities and strengths are what the company is looking for. Make it clear to the panel that you are the one for the job through your knowledge and interest in the company. If you don't already work for the company then the pressure on you will be less. The more you know about them the more they will be impressed!

BEING TOO MODEST

Failing to talk yourself up during an interview is one of the most self-defeating mistakes you can make. Of course, there is a fine line between confidence and arrogance but remember that you need to sell yourself. They are probably not aware of your achievements so make sure you tell them!

TALKING WAY TOO MUCH!

Be careful not to talk over the interviewer or interrupt when they are speaking. Those interviewees who lack in confidence and have not prepared are more likely to 'waffle' or talk about subjects they have no knowledge of. Sit calmly and listen carefully, answering questions thoughtfully.

DON'T CRITICISE YOUR PREVIOUS EMPLOYER

Even if you hated your former boss or felt your previous employer treated you unfairly, a job interview is not the place to express your feelings. The interview panel do not want to hear your grievances and you do not want to portray any bitterness during the interview (even if it is warranted). If you lost your previous job then be honest but always try to put a positive spin on the negative things that happened.

FAILING TO ASK RELEVANT QUESTIONS

Your CV may be impressive on paper, but employers also appreciate a candidate who can ask several intelligent questions at the end of the interview. Prepare at least 3 or 4 questions in advance to ask the interviewer. Make sure the questions are relevant and are not designed to make you look clever! Instead ask questions around development or opportunities. Avoid questions such as salary and leave.

SHOWING A LACK OF ENTHUSIASM

Having a positive attitude is vital and it all goes back to creating a first impression. Don't walk into the interview and make excuses about how bad your day is and that you might not perform well because of XYZ. Instead, be polite, courteous and upbeat. Show your enthusiasm for both the job and the opportunity to interview for it. And don't forget to thank the person at the end of the interview for their time!

FORGETTING THE FOLLOW-UP PLAN – PLAN B!

Make sure you send a handwritten thank you note or polite email to the interviewer expressing gratitude for his or her time and consideration (See section relating to PLAN B). However, don't start telephoning the company every day asking them if you've been successful or not. If they want you they will call you.

EXPLAIN WHY YOU LEFT YOUR LAST EMPLOYER

You may be in a position where you are 'in between' jobs. If this applies to you there is a possibility that you'll be asked the above question. If you are, then follow these simple guidelines when constructing your answer:

Describe the reason for your departure but don't go into specific details unless they ask you too. Make sure you provide references that support your reasons for leaving. Ensure that your reference includes specific details about your work performance. If you had a bad experience with your previous employer tell them briefly what happened. Ensure you stick to the facts and tell them what you would do differently next time. Never be negative about your previous employer, even if they treated you poorly.

Top Tip
Try, as hard it may be, to be positive about your previous employer. Remember the interviewer wants to hear good things about your current or previous employer.

CHAPTER 6:
PLAN B

WHAT IS A PLAN B?

I have sat on many interview panels where a candidate has interviewed well but has been narrowly beaten by another person. In these situations I always say to myself – "I may have a vacancy for them later on." Unfortunately when I call them up to give them the bad news they sometimes respond in a negative fashion and can even on occasions be abusive! I then say to myself – "I won't have a vacancy for them at a later stage." What I am trying to say here is that you should always have a PLAN B and understand that if you don't get a particular job the first time around you may get more than you bargained for at a later date. We recently had a case where a person had purchased this information guide and followed my advice to the letter. Unfortunately they didn't get the job the first time around but a few months later received a letter in the post offering them the chance to apply for another more senior position. Yes, you've guessed it; they got that job instead. They wrote to me thanking me for the following advice:

- If you don't get the job don't give up. If you are contacted by telephone with the bad news, by all means sound disappointed but not disheartened.

- Tell them (as hard as it may be) that you really enjoyed the interview and, if there are any more opportunities arising within the company in the future, could they let you know.

- Also tell them that you'd still really like to work for them.

You may be saying – "Why would I want to work for them after they didn't want me the first time?" but I always say that this kind of approach is counterproductive.

If someone is calling you to give you bad news they are expecting you to be disappointed and on some occasions annoyed. If they hear that you are positive and still upbeat in your response then they will remember you!

THE FOLLOW-UP LETTER

Immediately after your interview it is a good idea to follow up with a 'thank you' letter. This will serve a number of purposes. To begin with it will keep you at the forefront of the interview panel's minds and will also further demonstrate your thoughtful and appreciative nature.

Imagine if you were on the interview panel. At the end of the interview you have 3 people who are all as good as each other and could do a great job for you. The following day you receive a thank you letter from one of the 3 people. It tells you how much they enjoyed the interview and also reiterates the fact that they believe they would be a valuable asset to your company. Now who would you choose as the successful candidate?

On the following page I have provided you with a sample follow up letter. Use it as a guide for writing your own and try to address it personally to the chair of the interview panel.

SAMPLE FOLLOW-UP LETTER

Fiction Street,
Fiction Town,
Fiction.
FT1 1FT

Dear Mr Davies,

RE: INTERVIEW FOR CARE ASSISTANT POSTION/CAP 10987

I would like to take this opportunity to thank you for the interview that took place on the 11/01/2006. I very much enjoyed the experience and wanted to show my appreciation for you taking the time to see me.

I was impressed by the company's vision and believe that I would be a great asset to your organisation. In the meantime I look forward to hearing from you, but if I am not successful on this occasion please would you consider me for any future vacancies.

Once again thank you.

Yours sincerely,

Mr R McMunn

CHAPTER 7
HOW TO CREATE AN EFFECTIVE CV

During this section of the guide I will provide you with a step-by-step guide on how to create an effective CV. This will help you whenever you come to apply for a specific job in the future.

The word Curriculum Vitae translated means the 'course of life'. CVs are used to demonstrate to an employer that you have the potential, the skills, and the experience to carry out the role you are applying for. Your CV is a very important document and you should spend sufficient time designing it so that it matches the job that you are applying for as closely as possible.

WHAT MAKES AN EFFECTIVE CV?

In simple terms, an effective CV is one that matches the specification and the requirements of the job you are applying for. Your CV should be used as a tool to demonstrate that you have the right qualities and attributes to perform the role that you are applying for. It should primarily focus on:

- Creating the right impression of yourself;
- Indicating that you possess the right qualities and attributes to perform the role of the job you are applying for;
- Grabbing the assessor's attention;
- Being concise and clear.

The most effective CVs are the ones that make the assessor's job easy. They are simple to read, to the point, relevant and focus on the job/role that you are applying for. CVs should not be overly long unless an employer specifically asks for this. Effective CV writing is an acquired skill that can be obtained relatively quickly with a little bit of time, effort and focus.

Before you begin to start work on your CV it is a good idea to have a basic idea of how a job/person specification is constructed. A job description/ person specification is basically a blueprint for the role you are applying for; it sets out what the employer expects from potential applicants. One of your main focus points during the construction of your CV will be to match the job/person specification. Most job/person specifications will include the following areas:

EXPERIENCE REQUIRED: previous jobs, unpaid work experience, life experience, skills, knowledge and abilities: for example, languages, driving, knowledge of specialist fields, ability to use equipment, plus some indication of the level of competence required, and whether the person must have the skills or knowledge beforehand or can learn them on the job.

QUALIFICATIONS REQUIRED: exams, certificates, degrees, diplomas (some jobs require specific qualifications, but most do not and it can be fairer to ask for the skills or knowledge represented by the qualification rather than asking for the qualification itself).

PERSONAL ATTRIBUTES REQUIRED: such as strength, ability to lift, willingness to work in a hectic busy environment or on your own.

PERSONAL CIRCUMSTANCES: such as being able to work weekends or evenings or even to travel.

Most job/person specifications will be based around a task analysis of the vacancy, so there should be nothing within the job description/person specification that is irrelevant or that does not concern the particular role you are applying for. Whatever requirements you are asked to meet, you should try hard to match them as closely as possible, providing evidence if possible of your previous experience.

WHAT IS THE EMPLOYER LOOKING FOR IN YOUR CV?

Try to put yourself in the shoes of the employer. How would you want an applicant's CV to look? You would want it to be relevant to the role they are applying for and you would want it to be neat, concise and well organised.

For the majority of jobs there will be a job specification or person specification. You need to spend some time thinking about the type of person they are looking for and how you can match the specification that is relevant to the job you want. Most job specifications will list the essential/desirable requirements in terms of education, qualifications, training, experience, skills, personality and any other special requirements.

Let's take a look at some of the skills and qualifications required to become a Physical Training Instructor at a Sports Centre.

Qualifications required

You will need 2 GCSEs/SCEs or equivalent, in the subjects of English language at Grade C/3 minimum and in Mathematics at Grade G/6 minimum.

You will need to have a good standard of fitness in a number of sports and have the ability to swim.

You will be assessed via a specialist interview and be required to undertake additional tests.

About the job

Physical Training Instructors are responsible for organising and arranging physical fitness training programmes for members. Therefore a good standard of physical fitness and organisational skills are required. In addition to being physically fit you must also possess good motivational skills.

- Manage sporting facilities;
- Organise and conduct instructional classes;
- Perform fitness tests;
- Arrange and hold sports counselling sessions.

You will see from the above details that some of the key elements of the role include suitable levels of physical fitness, good organisational skills, motivational skills and the ability to manage people and resources. Once you have the above information then you will be able to mould your CV around the key aspects of the job.

Before I provide you with a sample CV that is based on matching the above role, let's first of all take a look at some of the key elements of a CV.

THE KEY ELEMENTS OF A CV

The following is a list of information I recommend you include within your CV. Try to put them in this order and remember to be brief and to the point. Make sure you include and highlight the positive aspects of your experience and achievements.

- **PERSONAL DETAILS**
- **PROFILE**
- **EMPLOYMENT HISTORY**
- **ACADEMIC ACIEVEMENTS**
- **INTERESTS**
- **ANY OTHER INFORMATION**
- **REFERENCES**

Let's now take a look at each of the above sections and what you need to include.

PERSONAL DETAILS

When completing this section you should include the following details:

- Your full name
- Address
- Date of birth
- Nationality
- Contact telephone numbers including home and mobile
- Email address

PROFILE

To begin with try to write a brief but to-the-point statement about yourself making sure you include the keywords that best describe your character. Some effective words to use when describing yourself might include:

Ambitious, enthusiastic, motivated, caring, trustworthy, meticulous, sense of humour, drive, character, determination, will to succeed, passionate, loyal, teamwork, hard working.

The above words are all powerful and positive aspects of an individual's character. Try to think of your own character and what positive words you can use that best describe you.

Within your profile description try to include a statement that is relative to you and that will make the assessor think you are the right person for the job, such as:

"I am an extremely fit and active person who has a great deal of experience in this field and I have a track record of high achievement. I have very good organisational and motivational skills and I am always striving to improve myself. I believe that I would embrace the challenges that this new role has to offer."

EMPLOYMENT HISTORY

When completing this section try to ensure that it is completed in reverse chronological order. Provide the reader with dates, locations and employers, and remember to include your job title. Give a brief description of your main achievements and try, again, to include words of a positive nature, such as:

Achieved, developed, progressed, managed, created, succeeded, devised, drove, expanded, directed.

It is also a good idea to quantify your main achievements, such as:

"During my time with this employer I was responsible for motivating my team and organising different activities."

ACADEMIC ACHIEVEMENTS

When completing this section include the dates, names and locations of the schools, colleges or universities that you attended in reverse chronological order.

You should also include your qualifications and any other relevant achievements such as health and safety qualifications or first aid qualifications. Anything that is relevant to the role you're applying for would be an advantage.

INTERESTS

Within this section try to include interests that match the requirements of the job and ones that also portray you in a positive manner. Maybe you have worked within the voluntary sector or have even carried out some charity work in the past? If so try to include these in your CV as they show you have a caring and concerning nature. You may also play sports or keep fit, in which case you should include these too. If you have any evidence of where you have worked effectively as part of a team then include this also.

ANY OTHER INFORMATION

Within this section of your CV you can include any other information that is relevant to your skills or experiences that you may feel are of benefit. Examples of these could be certificates of achievement from work or school.

REFERENCES

Although you will normally be required to provide two references as part of your application for a job, it is good practice to include these at the end of your CV. Try to include your current or previous employer, providing you know that they are going to write positive things about you. Be careful whom you choose as a reference and make sure you seek their permission first prior to putting down their name and contact details. It may also be a good idea to ask them if you can have a copy of what they have written about you for reference later.

SAMPLE CV

The following sample CV has been designed to give you an idea of how an effective CV might look. It has been created with the position of Physical Training Instructor in mind. All of the information provided is fictitious.

Curriculum Vitae of
Richard McMunn

Address: 75, Any Street, Anytown, Anyshire. ANY 123
Date of birth: 01/01/1970
Nationality: British
Telephone contact: 01227 XXXXX / Mobile 07890 XXX XXX
E-Mail contact: richardmcmunn@anyemailaddress.co.uk

Personal profile of
Richard McMunn

I am an extremely fit and active person who has a great deal of experience in this field and I have a track record of high achievement. I have very good organisational and motivational skills and I am always striving to improve myself. I believe that I would embrace the challenges that this new role has to offer. I am a motivated, dedicated, loyal and ambitious person who has the ability to work both within a team and also unsupervised.

I already have a large amount of experience in the working environment and take on a large number of responsibilities both at work, around the home and in my leisure time activities. I am currently the Captain of my local football team and part of my responsibilities includes organising and conducting weekly evening training sessions for the team. For every training session that I run I always try to vary the type of exercises that we perform. This allows me to maintain everyone's motivation and interest levels. For example, one week I will organise the Multi-Stage Fitness Test and another week we will practise tackling and dribbling skills.

To conclude, I am a fit, motivated active, organised and professional individual who has a lot of skills and experience to offer.

Employment history of
Richard McMunn
(in chronological order)

Job position/title/company #1
goes here

Date of employment
goes here

During my time with this employer I was responsible for motivating my team and organising different activities.

Job position/title/company #2
goes here

Date of employment
goes here

During my time with this employer I was responsible stock taking and dealing with customers' queries and complaints. I also took on the responsibility of arranging the company's annual staff leisure activity event, which often included some form of motivational talk.

Job position/title/company #3
goes here

Date of employment
goes here

During my time with this employer I undertook a training course in health and safety and first aid. Part of my role included managing resources and training rooms/equipment.

Academic achievements of
Richard McMunn

Health and Safety qualification	Date of achievement goes here
First Aid qualification	Date of achievement goes here
Level 1 Physical Training Instructor qualification	Date of achievement goes here
GSCE Maths Grade C	Date of achievement goes here
GCSE English Grade C	Date of achievement goes here
GCSE Physical Education Grade B	Date of achievement goes here

Interests and Hobbies of
Richard McMunn

I am an extremely fit and active person who carries out a structured training programme at my local gym five times a week. During my training sessions I will carry out a variety of different exercises such as indoor rowing, cycling, treadmill work and light weights. I measure my fitness levels by performing the multi-stage fitness test once a week and I can currently achieve level 14.5. In addition to my gym work I am a keen swimmer and break up my gym sessions with long swim sessions twice a week. I can swim 60 lengths of my local swimming pool in a time of 35 minutes.

I am also the Captain of my local football team and play in the position of midfield. I am also responsible for organising and arranging the weekly training sessions.

In addition to my sporting activities I like to relax with a weekly yoga group at my local community centre. I also have a keen interest in art and attend evening classes during the months of October through to December.

Further information

Six months ago I decided to carry out a sponsored fitness event in order to raise money for a local charity. I swam 60 lengths of my local swimming pool, and then ran 26 miles before cycling 110 miles all in one day. In total I managed to raise over £10,000 for charity.

References

Name, address and contact details of reference #1

Name, address and contact details of reference #2

TOP TIPS FOR CREATING AN EFFECTIVE CV

NEW APPLICATION = NEW CV

It is important that every time you apply for a job you re-evaluate the content of your CV so that you can match the skills and qualifications required. As a rule, you should complete a new CV for every job application unless your applications are close together and the job/person specification is relatively similar for each. Don't become complacent or allow your CV to get out of date.

DON'T PAD OUT YOUR CV

There is a common misconception amongst many job applicants that you need to make your CV scores of pages long for it to be recognised. This simply isn't true. When creating your CV aim for quality rather than quantity. If I was looking through an applicant's CV then I would much prefer to see 2 pages of high quality focused information rather than 5 pages padded out with irrelevance.

CREATE A POSITIVE IMAGE

Writing an effective CV involves a number of important aspects. One of those is the manner in which you present your CV. When developing your CV ask yourself the following questions:

- Is your spelling, grammar and punctuation correct?
- Is it legible and easy to read?
- Is the style in which you are writing your CV standardised?
- Is it neat?
- Is it constructed in a logical manner?

By following the above tips in respect of your CV image you will be on the right track to improving your chances of getting the job you are after. You should spend just as much time on the **presentation** of your CV as you do on the **content**.

DO YOU HAVE THE RIGHT QUALITIES AND ATTRIBUTES FOR THE JOB YOU ARE APPLYING FOR?

When you are developing your CV have a look at the required personal qualities that are listed within the job/person spec. Try to match these as closely as possible but, again, ensure that you provide examples where appropriate. For example, in the sample job description for a Physical Training Instructor, one of the required personal qualities was to:

'Organise and conduct instructional classes'

Try to provide an example of where you have achieved this in any previous roles. The following is a fictitious example of how this might be achieved:

"I am currently the Captain of my local football team and part of my responsibilities include organising and conducting weekly evening training sessions for the team. For every training session that I run I always try to vary the type of exercises that we perform. This allows me to maintain everyone's motivation and interest levels. For example, one week I will organise the Multi-Stage Fitness Test for them and another week I will arrange practice tackling and dribbling skills."

Matching your qualities and attributes to the role you are applying for is very important.

BE HONEST WHEN CREATING YOUR CV

If you lie on your CV, especially when it comes to academic qualifications or experience, you will almost certainly get caught out at some point in the future. Maybe not straight away but even a few months or years down the line an employer can still dismiss you for incorrect information that you provide during the selection process. It simply isn't worth it. Be honest when creating your CV and if you don't have the right skills for the job you are applying for, then go out there and get them!